UNGOVERNED HUNGER : *How*
Unchecked Appetite Dismantles Authority

by Dr. Marlene Miles

Freshwater Press 2026

Freshwaterpress9@gmail.com

ISBN: 978-1-971933-10-8

Paperback Version

Table of Contents

UNGOVERNED HUNGER

How Unchecked Appetite Dismantles Authority

Freshwater

HUNGER IS NOT A GAME

Hunger is not a game, and neither is it a problem as God established things. God created food before He created man. He created vegetation on Day 3, sea creatures and birds on Day 5. Then on Day 6, He created land animals and then *formed* man.

> Be not ye therefore like unto them, for your Father knoweth what things ye have need of before ye ask Him. (Matthew 6:8)

Before you ask, the Lord already knows what you have need of. If we've asked and still don't have, then the issue may be that we are asking amiss--, either for the wrong thing, asking at the wrong time, asking incorrectly, or any combination of the aforementioned.

All the answers of God are Yes, and Amen. So where are our yeses?

Jehovah Jireh, the Lord Our Provider. For those who may not have been born into a family with a father who was a true provider, I want to speak on that for a moment. A man takes honor in taking care of his family; it is his joy. And it gives him Godly pride to know that he is *providing*. There are men or parents who do not have that temperament or ability, and it usually frustrates them to distraction. Still, ladies, I'm talking to you, you should marry a provider. I am not talking about a man's bank account or economic status. Providing is a mindset, it is a gift, it is his joy and good pleasure, it is his *calling* or at least a part of his calling. The man is empowered to do it. However, the man who himself is **hungry**, seemingly or perpetually hungry is an *owned* man and therefore he is not and cannot become a provider as he is.

There is hope though. He <u>can</u> become a provider, but he must be restored into that position. So that his joy again is good stewardship and providing. Like God; he got it from God.

God provided everything for mankind before man was ever formed. Ever. God provided a place and also provision, that is, food to eat. God knew we would have hunger, so before we ever needed food or asked, He provided. He is Our

Provider. I am not saying that it is sin to have children that you cannot or will not take care of, but I am saying it is not the model that God showed us, even in the Beginning.

Not only was sustenance provided, it was provided abundantly. Until the Fall of Man. God had said, of the Tree of the Knowledge of Good and Evil, thou shalt not eat.

Right there is where we learn that hunger is expected, and God has already answered and already provided, therefore we should not have any anxiety about it. That is one of the first yeses and amens. Provision has been ordered, like everything God does. On Day 1 of Creation God began to set order out of darkness and void. We serve a God of order and discipline. Order was set in how to eat, what to eat and what not to eat.

When it comes to knowledge, God provided it. When it comes to the knowledge of good and evil, the devil provided that. Have you ever wondered if Adam and Eve were getting the 'knowledge of good and evil', then how did they make such an uninformed choice to trade authority for 'fruit"?

In the Book of Genesis, knowledge does not mean Wisdom, maturity, discernment, or

7

authority. It means experiential awareness, empirical knowledge. In Hebrew thought, *to know* is not to understand abstractly, it is to enter into experience. The knowledge of good and evil is not just knowing what good and evil *are; it is* bearing awareness of both; and by way of the Serpent it was attained without Godly governance.

The choice to eat of this forbidden tree wasn't informed. Since Adam and Eve did not trade authority *after* understanding the cost; the cost was hidden from them before they decided. They traded authority <u>before</u> they had the capacity to **govern** what they were receiving.

They had innocence, alignment, authority, covering, and access. What they *lacked* was tested discernment, consequence-bearing wisdom, and restraint under pressure. So, the temptation wasn't, "Do you want evil?" No, it was, "Do you want access without waiting?" And, the devil is still asking men that question.

That's appetite, not ignorance.

They did not gain authority, Wisdom, rule, or dominion. They gained self-awareness without covering, moral consciousness without governance, and perception without capacity.

Scripture says, *Be wise in what is good, and innocent in what is evil. Do not gain evil through experience.*

WHEN HUNGER IS NOT GOVERNED

Man broke that order when the woman stepped outside obedience, and Adam followed her into disobedience.

We will get to this more later, but the order that God established was based on obedience, on discipline, or rules, and on authority. Man, in the earth, like a colony in the Garden of Eden was under the auspices and authority of God. When man decided to disobey, he stepped out from his God given authority, like stepping out of a garment. He willingly took it off. He willingly laid down his God-given glory, and we know this because he was now naked and ashamed, so he began to hide.

We know he took off glory because you cannot hide glory. Even the glory that is due man cannot be hid under a bushel. We know this because the Glory of God is so great, that Moses could only see a bit of it as the Lord went by, while Moses was safely in the cleft of the rock.

The glory of a man is his authority. The authority of a man is his glory.

Man was not created in low estate. Man was not crated and placed in survival mode. Men of low estate live in survival mode. Or rather, survival mode produces low-estate living. Men of higher estate live differently, not because they necessarily have more resources, but because they understand authority and guard it. Men of low estate seek to stay alive. Men of higher estate seek to remain governed.

Men of low estate live in survival mode. Or, survival mode puts men into low-estate living. Men of higher estate live differently not so much that they have more money or more means, but they think differently. A man of higher estate understands authority and he guards it. Men of low estate just want to stay alive and that usually starts with food.

PROVISION KEEPS MAN ALIVE

There is a man who is always asking for provision. Then there is another man who as graduated to asking about authority. Two Men. Two Questions. Two Stages.

The dominant question of the man asking for provision is, "Will this meet my need?" He is governed by appetite, urgency, lack (real or perceived). He is ever relief-seeking, so he asks things like: *Will you help me? Can you provide? What do I get out of this? Will this sustain me?*

This man is not evil, but he is vulnerable, because provision without authority always comes with terms.

Provision, and that alone will keep a man alive, but then he arises the next day and things are the same because he isn't in authority, he is only alive. His body is alive, but his authority is not under his own control. When a man has to take off and lay down the very thing that will get him **out** of a place in order to step into that place, he has undone himself. He cannot get out of that place without the thing that he traded, exchanged, or relinquished. It's like the cost of rowing to a remote island is the very boat that transported you there. How will you ever leave the island?

Sometimes that very needed thing is removed by trickery or force. Joseph's coat was taken from him, yet that coat would have identified him, if not as Jacob's son, the son of a prince, but at least a person of wealth and position. Had Joseph been in that coat, the Midianites may not have bought him as a slave; nor would they have sold him again in Egypt.

That coat represented Joseph's authority, but it was removed from him. Without his voice, his authority and position, the thing that he needed to get him out of the pit and back home to his own father, had been taken from him. Joseph was sold as a slave; he became *owned.*

THE LIE OF *"JUST ENOUGH"*

Many men believe that once immediate or pressing problems are solved, or a certain situation is handled, promotion will follow. Progress is assumed to be automatic after he is comfortable or not stressed. Movement is expected as a reward for endurance. That assumption is not God's order.

When man has rejected God's order and chosen his own way, leaning to his own desires or understanding, he has allowed his flesh to make the decision. Flesh will take over and make the choice because the man is trying to stay alive, **right now**. The flesh is always **right now.** Flesh order is not how God established things at all. It is a distortion, a perversion, a twisting of sequence.

This may come as a shock to everyone who has ever been a baby or a child, had a parent, or been on a date: God's order was never to solve hunger first. God's order is not to settle hunger first and then later that man will gain authority.

God's order as man walks in authority, in that pattern, that man's hunger remains governed.

The devil's work has always been to reverse order. Order is foundational so if order is scrambled, there is no sure foundation. In Eden, God gave man a garden. Food was already present. Provision was abundant. The ground cooperated with man. Appetite existed there, but it was not dominant.

The Serpent did not introduce hunger; he introduced menu anxiety. Through repeated suggestion, he reframed abundance as insufficiency. He implied that what God had provided was somehow incomplete, outdated, or limiting. Maybe he said there was not enough variety, but he really leaned into there is not enough *experience.* I know grown folk today who are still looking for *experiences;* the world will comply, and bring them much trouble.

The Serpent may have said something like, Eat something different. Eat something more. Eat something now. And with that shift, man stepped out of place, out of order, out of provision and out from under covering.

Outside the Garden, the ground no longer cooperated with man. Provision became laborious. Sustenance replaced abundance. Appetite moved to the foreground, while authority slipped quietly into the background.

This same distortion followed Israel into the wilderness. The Israelites were not starving because God sustained them. Yet, God's sustenance was no longer enough for *appetite* that they had become accustomed to. This is what happens with experiences, when you final get where you are supposed to be you've got memories of things that you never should have done or experienced. So, in the Wilderness they began to complain. Manna was despised not because it failed, but because it did not **entertain**.

The people rehearsed memories of garlic, leeks, and cucumber. These were foods associated with captivity. In so doing, they trained themselves to resent what was sustaining them. Manna was clean by design. It was given to break their appetite for Pharaoh's delicacies. It would have worked had they submitted to God's process.

No, they didn't submit; they kept complaining.

Then, they asked for meat. God gave it to them, not as a reward, but as exposure. He allowed appetite to have its way, and it made them sick. The problem was never food. The problem was that **appetite** had been allowed to govern.

The Lord is my Shepherd: I shall not want.

Those who have been babies or children may have heard your parents asking you, probably over and again, *"What do you want?"* They thought it was love. No, that was training the appetite to rule.

The *apple* in the Garden had primed the well of dissatisfaction, but man called it hunger. When any man sins, that is worship to the false idol that led him to sin. The first thing that idol does is to give his sin nature to that man. The serpent installed *dissatisfaction* into man that day. That was the trade, and it was a lousy trade.

This is the lie of *just enough*: From then on it's as though man is saying, If I can just get through this season, I'll move forward. If I can just solve this one thing, progress will follow. If I can just be sustained a little longer, change will come. But sustenance is not movement. Relief is not release. Being kept alive is not the same as being advanced.

Scripture asks the question plainly: Why have men made their bellies into *gods? Why have they made their bellies into* things that must

17

be pleased, tended to, negotiated with — and yet are never satisfied?

Because appetite, once unguided, does not lead forward. It keeps men circling. *Just enough* keeps hunger temporarily relieved, but also engaged. *Just enough* delays authority Just enough makes captivity feel reasonable. This is why so many remain where they are, alive, sustained, fed, and yet unmoved. Have you ever fed a stray animal? It comes back to that same spot over and again; it doesn't move on.

They are not stuck because God withheld. They are stuck because appetite was used in attempt to manage authority. Isn't this right up there with using a leaf to cover nakedness and shame? So, we see the "knowledge" they got was useless to get them out of the predicament they put themselves in by making the first trade. And the first trade required their authority; the very thing that would get them out of the predicament that the trade would put them in.

Men think that as soon as they get this problem solved or that problem solved then they will be promoted or progress in life. Man has chosen the order. Well, he has let his flesh choose it. The order is not how God established order at all. God's order has been distorted, perverted, twisted. The devil did that. God gave man the Garden at Eden. The food was already there. Somehow the devil, through his repeated infomercials, even before TV, convinced Eve that she needed something different to eat. The enemy repeatedly reframed what was already provided until desire began to feel like lack. That got them and us under the Curse of the Law and put out of place and provision. Outside the Garden at Eden the ground wasn't blessed and working for mankind. Inside the Garden, it was. After all their complaining, God let the Israelites in the Wilderness have the WFQ a Wilderness Free Quail buffet – *ad nauseum* and for punishment. Both times, appetite was ruling.

Man has been looking for comfort food ever since Eden because comfort was displaced; satisfaction was removed and replaced with *dissatisfaction*.

What was lost when glory (covering, weight, authority, *Presence*) was removed, man lost settledness, safety without striving, identity without performance, comfort without consumption. That loss created unease, not just hunger.

Appetite stepped in to try to soothe what authority used to secure. Authority means being close to God, so now the relationship is strained or gone. But if man doesn't realize any of that, he just eats not just to live, but to self-soothe, quiet anxiety, recreate safety, simulate *Presence*, dull exposure. That's comfort. Whether it's food, money, sex, work, noise, control, or even religion. Then he believes after he is satisfied – and without God, he never will be, but after becoming satisfied **he** will solve the rest of his problems.

Himself. But he cannot do it. Himself.

It never works because comfort food is temporary relief trying to compensate for a permanent spiritual absence. It calms, but it does not cover. It soothes, but it does not govern. It fills the mouth, but does not compensate for the weight of Glory that has been displaced. So, the cycle continues. Man has been eating for comfort ever since he lost covering. Comfort food is what we reach for when glory is gone.

That explains addiction, compulsion, excess, and even boredom in the place of abundance. It explains why 'enough' never satisfies.

Relief numbs absence; authority restores *Presence. Men are owned when comfort replaces governance.*

HOW MEN ARE OWNED

Snack chips & ice cream fit the appetite problem. Some of us have a favorite snack chip. You take a bite and recognize the flavor immediately—but it's never quite enough. So, you eat another, and then another, chasing the satisfaction you expect to arrive. But it never does. The full authority of that flavor was never in the bag.

That flavor sensation is intermittent reward. This mirrors casino logic, relational appetite, and provision traps. Appetite chases what authority never intends to give. Some things are designed to keep you reaching, yet never ruling.

I was "attached' to a certain ice cream for a long time until I realized it was a flavor that I enjoyed every so often as a kid when I would go to the store with my dad. In repeatedly seeking out this particular ice cream, I was trying to rehearse the memory. The flavor was close, but it wasn't satisfying me in the present. It was summoning a moment from the past. I wasn't eating simply for pleasure, I was revisiting and trying to recreate something impossible to recreate because I could not turn back time. Appetite will disguise anything, even childhood longings. I was not chasing flavor, although I thought I was. I was touching time, but as soon as I realized it, I no longer needed that ice cream.

Before that realization, I was *owned* by that ice cream.

When Adam and Eve sinned, in addition to whatever else happened, a spiritual wound was opened where the glory that is due man was drawn out. Now he has a vacated glory space that he caused. There was a loss of covering, weight, and governance. In place of it was a rush of appetite. Appetite is man's idea, man's understanding of what will fix this emptiness problem.

When Adam disobeyed, nothing was added to him that he was meant to carry; but his glory was taken from him. That was not the agreement though; man was supposed to have installed in him, the 'knowledge of good and evil.' But what he really gained was exposure.

When his eyes were opened, shame entered, and hiding began. What he lost was covering; then man tried to cover his shame. His improvisation didn't work.

Glory is covering, weight, and governance. Biblically, glory is not sparkle; it is weight. It is *Presence*. It is authority made visible. It says, *Look who I look like. Look at Who I belong to.* Without glory, man is well---, nobody.

When Adam stepped out from obedience, he stepped out from authority, governance, and divine covering.

Nature abhors a vacuum. Where there is nothing where there should be something-- , something else will rush to fill that spot. That glory-space in man didn't disappear; it became vacant. God knows what belongs there. The devil wants to fill it with something counterfeit. And man thinks, hmm, food or some other activity, comfort or passion may satisfy this emptiness.

Appetite became insatiable because things related to appetite are natural things: food, beverage, things of this world, fame, power, wealth. Therefore, it cannot *fill* identity because identity comes from God. Appetite was designed to respond to provision under authority.

Once authority was gone, appetite was promoted to a role it cannot perform. So now the eyes are never satisfied, the stomach is never full, acquisition never settles, and experience never completes. These objects are being asked to do the job of glory. And nothing can do the job of Glory, but Glory.

The eye is not satisfied with seeing, nor the ear filled with hearing. (Ecclesiastes 1:8)

The enemy did not convince Eve she lacked food. He convinced her she lacked completion. This was an attack on God, but that's not what Eve heard. The devil kept talking and eventually he reframed fullness as deficiency. That is the first lie of appetite, saying something such as, *What you have is not enough to make you whole.*

Once that lie lands, appetite becomes urgent, and urgency bypasses governance when man believed that it was worth trading authority for this fake completeness. This is way more than stress eating.

Nothing else ever works after man believes that lie, well – not until he stops believing it. After that lie, man keeps trying to put things into a space that was designed to be filled by the *Presence* of God, by the Holy Spirit. The legitimate operating system of man is the Holy Spirit of God.

You can eat food. You can accumulate wealth. You can collect experiences. You can acquire power. But none of those have **weight**. Glory has weight. Authority has weight. *Presence* has weight.

Appetite does not carry *Presence* or weight. Even if you gain weight from appetite, that's not the same thing as the weight of Glory, or the glory that is due man.

So, the cycle becomes: fill oneself to feel relief. Later on, one will feel empty and then fill again--, with something new, something else, something more, even more *experiences*. Man is trying to restore weight with consumption. And like a baby, man too often thinks that everything goes in his mouth.

Men are owned when appetite was promoted to replace Glory--, which is impossible. Ownership doesn't begin with chains. It begins with vacancy. And whatever fills the vacancy becomes the governor. That's how men are owned.

Men are rarely owned by force. They are owned by agreement. Ownership does not begin with chains or cages. It begins with an internal vacancy. A space once governed by authority, is now managed by appetite. After the Fall, man became uncovered. Once dark things began to fill his vacancy, he became owned with very real tendency to become evil, depending on who was now governing him.

What left man was not desire, but glory — the weight of God's *Presence* that ordered his inner world. When that covering was removed, something essential went missing: settledness. Authority. The quiet assurance of being held in place.

That absence created unease; appetite rushed in to do a job it was never designed to perform. Appetite was never meant to govern. It was meant to respond under authority, within order. But once authority was laid down, appetite was promoted.

Appetite cannot rule; it can only demand. This is the beginning of ownership.

Ownership of man begins with vacancy. The enemy did not convince man he lacked food, he convinced him he lacked something necessary to be complete. Man, either decided that was food, or he was led to believe it was food that was missing.

The first lie of ownership is not scarcity. It is deficiency of self. Once a man believes something essential is missing inside him, he will begin to negotiate with anything that promises relief. Hunger becomes urgent. Urgency narrows discernment. And whatever answers hunger begins to govern allegiance.

This is how ownership enters quietly, through comfort more easily than cruelty.

Comfort is a poor governor. Man has been searching for comfort food ever since he lost covering. Not just food, but anything that soothes. Comfort temporarily calms the sensation of exposure, by distraction, really, but it does not restore authority. It quiets anxiety, but it does not re-cover the soul. So, the relief fades quickly, and appetite returns louder than before. This explains a number of things: a fasted belly can 'hear' God; a full one usually does not, or not as clearly.

The settling, and then the quick return of appetite is why the eye is never satisfied. This is why the ear is never filled, why "enough" never arrives and never settles.

Ownership of a man does not require cruelty. It requires need. Once appetite is ungoverned, just give that man things for his appetite; even bad things, things that would hurt him or even kill.

The enticement is easy: *Just this once. Until things get better. I'll stop later. I have no other option. I need this. I deserve this. This will fix it.*

Provision without authority always comes with conditions. Not because the provider is evil, but because hunger weakens position. A man who needs relief now and trades it for appetite cannot negotiate for tomorrow because he lost his authority **in the trade**. Once he agrees, he trades. He yields ground. Even though his appetite satisfies him for the time being, or temporarily, over time, what he agreed to begins to own him. And he may have completely forgotten that he made that trade or why he made that trade. He just knows things that used to work in his life no longer work.

What needs to work for a man to progress and be successful in life is his **authority. Without authority a man is owned.** Ownership is difficult to recognize because it feels reasonable at first. It often feels like survival, practicality, Wisdom, patience, realism, but survival mode is not neutral. It slowly reassigns governance.

A man who lives only to stay alive will eventually give up what would have gotten him out. Provision keeps him breathing. Authority would have moved him forward. But authority requires restraint, waiting, and trust, and these are all the things *appetite* works against.

Men are not owned because they are weak, they are owned because appetite was asked to replace authority. Chains are not required. That man is owned; vacancy is enough. And this is the mechanism: When authority leaves, appetite takes over. When appetite governs, ownership follows.

WHEN MEN ARE OWNED

The man who keeps eating and eating (not just food), -- if he is being fed and fed and constantly needs to be fed, he is either a baby or a prisoner. We must know when the enemy is feeding a prisoner versus the man having enough agency to get his own provisions and desires. Or is there no line between?

The line is that thing you won't cross because it will compromise you. The thing you are not willing to trade or lose is: agency.

Babies are fed because they cannot govern. Prisoners are fed so they cannot leave. There are two reasons someone is fed repeatedly. A baby is fed because authority has not yet formed. A baby has no agency, cannot provide, cannot leave, cannot steward restraint. Feeding a baby may be merciful and formative, but there still could be an agenda. The Godly goal is growth into agency.

From infancy and childhood, feeding decreases over time as strength increases, responsibility grows, self-governance develops, or the extraction is complete and the person is no longer considered useful to the "feeder."

If feeding leads toward independence, it is parental.

A prisoner is fed so authority never forms. He is fed to be kept alive, sustained. He is not to be released, and he is not taught to govern. He may be brainwashed or lied to for the purpose of making him do the opposite of governing. Feeding here is containment, not care.

Serpent in the Garden territory? The goal is not growth for governance; the goal is maintenance without movement. If feeding repeats without producing agency, it is custodial.

The enemy's feeding is never nurturing. A parent can give a child everything they want and that is not nurturing. So it doesn't matter who is doing what, it matters *what* they are doing, and to what end. The enemy does not feed to mature; he feeds to pacify. His provision shuts the captive up, quiets resistance, manages unrest, prevents desperation and removes urgency to escape. This is why relief comes quickly, satisfaction fades fast, dependency increases (you want more of what you cannot get for yourself), movement never happens. It's not starvation; it's **controlled sustenance**.

Here's how to tell the difference. **Feeding that forms a <u>son</u>** increases discernment, teaches, produces restraint, leads to self-governance, reduces urgency, and widens future options. Feeding that creates or maintains a prisoner increases appetite, dulls discernment, requires repetition, narrows options, delays movement. The question is not *"Am I being fed? The question is,* "Is this feeding increasing my capacity to govern, or dependency, my need to be <u>fed again</u>?"

The line is crossed when provision replaces authority, when relief delays release, when feeding removes the need to decide and when appetite manages time and attention. At that point, the man is no longer being nurtured; he is being **managed**.

There can be a gray area during transition. There can be moments when a man is being sustained by God while authority is still forming, before release is possible. In those seasons pressure still teaches, restraint is required, appetite is not indulged, and it is obvious that governance is increasing.

> But speaking the truth in love, may grow up into him in all things, which is the head, even Christ: (Ephesians 4:15)

If feeding comes without *formation*, it is not from God; we all should be growing and growing up in Him. Feeding that produces agency is fathering. Feeding that prevents agency is imprisonment. When being fed makes you stronger, it's nurture. If being fed makes you dependent, it's captivity.

A man who *can* govern but doesn't will always be fed like a prisoner, not because he lacks ability, but because he surrendered authority. So, pretending you can't when you can is the same as the man who knows to do, but won't; it is sin. There are too many who want free stuff, free food – anything free. But there are no free lunches; everything comes with a price. Some place themselves on lists and sponsorships to 'get over', but they are losing governance and becoming owned day by day.

Babies grow out of feeding. Prisoners live on it. Appetite cannot tell the difference, so the man must, and only governance can.

Laban owned Jacob for so many years, gave him just enough to keep him right there. That was ownership-by-provision, Scripture shows Laban's ownership without chains, without starvation, and without overt cruelty. That's the most dangerous kind.

Laban owned Jacob (mechanically, not morally). Laban did not keep Jacob by force. He kept him by calibrated provision and appetite. Jacob wanted Rachel. Jacob was fed, sheltered, married- getting his sexual needs met. He was also productive, but he was not free. Laban repeatedly changed Jacob's wages, adjusted terms after agreement, restructured outcomes midstream, benefited disproportionately. Yet, Jacob stayed.

Why?

Because provision was always *just enough* to delay departure, and appetite (for Rachel especially) was still active. This is ownership, not employment. Employment increases agency, clarifies terms, leads toward independence.

Ownership moves goalposts, rewards endurance without advancement, keeps wages low and keeps the future vague. It makes leaving feel risky.

Laban's genius (and wickedness) was not so much cruelty as it was containment. Jacob wasn't starving; he was stalled.

Jacob stayed so long because he was positionally compromised. He had no land, no inheritance. Well--, not *yet*. He had family responsibilities, and increasing dependents. Jacob thought he would work his way out of this set up; oh, not so. Appetite (and obligation) governed timing.

Leaving felt irresponsible; staying felt practical, and that's how ownership works.

Owned men are not starved, they are sustained. They have enough food to survive. Enough reward to hope. Enough comfort to delay, but not enough authority to exit.

God Had to Intervene. Provision did not lead Jacob out. Negotiation did not free him.

Hard work did not end it. Only restored authority did. On top of that, when Jacob finally left, Laban chased him, accused him, and tried to reassert control. Why? Because ownership resists release.

Laban didn't mentor or nurture Jacob; he used him. Laban didn't starve Jacob; he sustained Jacob just enough to keep him. Ownership doesn't have to look like cruelty, although it can. Ownership looks like provision without progress. When provision replaces authority, when you have to shut your mouth or shut down your own plans to exist or feed appetite, ownership is already present. That's called, *bought and paid for*. That is when you're on someone's payroll and you're not going anywhere, not because you don't want to, but because it wouldn't make sense and wouldn't look right if you did. When a man gets enough to stay but doesn't have enough to leave. That is when a man is owned.

Laban is a pattern of *kind* ownership.

BUY ME BACK

Buy me back from wherever they have sold me is a prayer point I have used and am not shy about using. But what if *they* is you?

So, the worst person to sell a man is that man himself? The most effective seller of a man is the man himself. The fact that a man can sell himself means that at the time of sale, that man has control of his own authority; he has agency. Else, he would not be able to close the sale.

Self-sale is the worst kind. no external seller can move a man as efficiently as his own appetite. An outside oppressor has to threaten, coerce, restrict, monitor. But when a man sells himself, none of that is needed.

When a man sees, yes, there go those eyes again, something he wants, his appetite is stimulated again and there he goes, negotiating, bargaining. Folks, flesh and blood and the human mind is no match for spiritual bargaining with unseen entities, contracts and generational covenants with fine and fine-fine print.

He rationalizes the terms, explains away the cost, calls delay Wisdom, misnames captivity, calling it, prudence. Ownership becomes self-maintaining. Appetite writes the contract when appetite governs, the man supplies the justification, the timing, the concessions, the renewal clauses.

Scripture shows so many exchanges that *look* voluntary: Esau, Judas, Jacob (before awakening), Israel in the wilderness. No one dragged them; they agreed. Yet, this is so dangerous. A man sold by another knows he is owned, but a man who sells himself believes he is *choosing*. That belief delays awakening.

The Law is that no one can own a man who refuses to agree. But a man who agrees does not need an owner. That's not blame, that's agency. Agency is actually good news because what is sold by agreement can be reclaimed by order, not force.

No one sells a man as cheaply as his own appetite. The worst trafficker is nside the gate. When a man sells himself, no chains are required.

Judas Iscariot thought he was selling Jesus. But he sold himself. Judas thought he was trading access to Jesus for silver, proximity to power for a payout of momentary leverage that would bring Judas relief. He believed the transaction was isolated and *external (I mean, who would know?) but what* actually changed was not what Judas thought would change.

Jesus' authority was not diminished, but Judas' governance was. The sale didn't transfer Jesus' power; it reassigned Judas' allegiance. From that moment, appetite and urgency governed Judas and as we look at his quick spiral we can see this clearly.

You can't sell what you don't own. Judas never owned Jesus' authority. But he did own his own obedience, so, ultimately, that's what he surrendered. That's why the money brought no peace, regret came without repentance, and returning the silver changed nothing. It did not nullify the deal. The transaction was already complete.

When a man thinks he's selling someone else, if that man has no guile or iniquity in him, no cause that he could be or should be sold, then the would-be vendor is usually selling himself. Judas transferred his own governance.

APPETITE AS A TRANSFER OF AUTHORITY

Authority does not disappear when it is abandoned; it is transferred. They assume authority is either possessed or lost, held or gone. But Scripture shows something more precise: authority moves. And it almost always moves at the point of appetite.

Appetite is not neutral. It is directional. What a man reaches for in hunger quietly determines who governs him next.

Appetite is an exchange point. Hunger creates urgency. Urgency narrows options. Narrowed options invite agreements that would never be made in fullness. This is not manipulation; it is mechanics. When appetite governs decision-making, authority shifts from discernment to relief, patience to urgency, position to survival. And the moment a man allows appetite to decide *for him*, he has already yielded governance.

That is the transfer.

Appetite is effective because it is all about timing. It says, *now, quickly, just this once, and you'll fix it later.* It does not deny authority; it simply postpones it. Just so you know, postponed authority is still surrendered authority. This is why appetite is such a reliable lever. It does not require deception, only pressure.

A man under pressure will trade tomorrow for today without calling it betrayal. He will call it necessity.

Appetite gives the illusion of choice. Men often say, *"I chose this."* And in one sense, they did. But appetite compresses the field of vision so tightly that the choice no longer includes long-term consequences, authority preservation, and future position. So, the decision is voluntary. But it is not free.

Freedom requires governance. Appetite removes governance, at the price of freedom. This is how authority moves without noise or resistance. This will move a man from sonship to servitude, and he may not even know it happened.

When authority transfers through appetite, sonship erodes quietly.

The man does not stop believing; he does not stop functioning. He does not stop participating. He simply stops governing.

He simply stops governing, and he didn't even know that his scepter? crown? signet ring? whatever represented his authority was gone??? He didn't *throw authority away* in a dramatic moment. He stopped governing, and authority slipped off him quietly.

When Tamar asks Judah for a pledge, she does not ask for money, she asks for his signet ring, his cord, his staff (walking stick). Each item represents authority. The signet ring authenticated documents, represented identity and was his personal seal. This is symbolic in that Judah gave up his seal, meaning he was no longer "sealed" at that time. To give the signet ring was to temporarily hand over the right to act in your own name. That is relinquishing authority even if it is considered temporary.

Judah didn't just promise payment. He surrendered representation. (My question is, why didn't King Judah have enough money for the transaction? He knew where he was going and what he would do there, *right*?)

The Cord held the signet, symbolizing continuity, and lineage. This wasn't jewelry; it was infrastructure. Taking the cord meant Tamar had the means to display and prove authority, not just possess it privately. The Staff (walking stick) symbolized leadership and jurisdiction. Judah handed over his visible symbol of governance. He did all this for sex.

The exchange was appetite-driven, Judah was quite hungry, it seems--, sexually, emotionally, situationally. Appetite does what it always does, it trades long-term authority for immediate relief. In that moment: Judah was not governing himself. his authority idled and became easily transferable, while he was distracted.

When authority is not being governed, it becomes transferable. Ungoverned authority does not vanish — it changes hands. Judah didn't stop being Judah. But for a moment, his authority was out of his control. Judah handed over the symbols of rule because he had stopped ruling himself. Judah had given himself some down-time and taken himself *off the clock.*

Authority is lost more often by neglect than rebellion. Most men do not wake up and say, *"I relinquish my authority." Instead, t*hey defer decisions to appetite. They postpone restraint, trade patience for relief, or allow urgency to decide. When that happens, authority, which requires active governance, simply... leaves. It leaves because it is no longer being exercised. Use it or lose it.

Judah didn't seem to notice because authority is symbolic *and* functional.

Symbols of authority include a scepter which is, authority exercised. The crown exemplifies authority recognized. The signet ring indicates when authority is delegated.

Authority does not announce its departure. Life still works. Provision still comes. People still respond--, well, at least for a while. So, the man assumes nothing has changed.

Appetite, ungoverned hunger is the perfect distraction. The strategy is, *Let's give him something he wants* and while he's busy managing hunger, relief, survival, or comfort, he doesn't notice that his decisions no longer carry weight. his words no longer stabilize environments. When does he finally realize that his presence no longer orders chaos. He still *exists* in the role, but he no longer **governs** it. So, the symbols are gone. The crown is gone, the signet ring is missing, and the scepter is no longer in his hand. But because nothing collapses immediately, he doesn't know it.

He simply stops governing.

There's no rebellion, no drama, no hatred. Just neglect, and neglect is enough to lose authority. Authority is rarely taken by force; it is usually laid down unnoticed. By the time he noticed the crown was gone, he had already stopped ruling. Authority doesn't leave with noise; It leaves when governance does. that's why so many don't know when it's gone.

RULE *little k*, king or get off the throne.

There is no such thing as partial governance. You are either ruling (actively governing), or not ruling. Not ruling is vacating the throne (even if you're still sitting in the chair)

Authority does not tolerate passivity. If you are not in right authority in your own house and now your kids are ruling the roost --- well. *Little-k* king" acknowledges *delegated* authority (not sovereignty). A *little-k* king still must rule. Delegated authority still requires governance.

If he doesn't rule, something else will. Both nature and spiritual realms abhor vacuums. So, the throne does not stay empty.

Appetite sits there. Fear sits there. Comfort sits there. Urgency sits there. So, if the king (of any variety) is not ruling then he/she is yielding the seat. A throne is never empty. Rule — or step aside. Govern — or abdicate.

If the *little k* king was using his authority, he would have known that it was either under threat or taken. There is inherent protection in the gifts and authority that God gives us WHEN it is working.

Authority in use is self-revealing. A man who is governing knows when resistance increases, pressure rises, boundaries are challenged, alignment is tested.

Authority in operation encounters friction and it is felt. It is answered. It is contested. *If he had been using it*, he would have known it was under threat. Silence is not neutral; it's diagnostic.

Authority and all spiritual gifts carry inherent protection when functioning. God-given authority is not fragile when it is rightly ordered, actively governed, being used within its assignment. When authority is functioning it resists encroachment, it produces clarity, it draws appropriate boundaries, it exposes challengers early.

That's why Scripture repeatedly shows authority being recognized, not defended. Storms quiet. Demons identify rank. Creation responds.

Authority doesn't scramble to protect itself; order does that.

Authority wasn't taken *from* Judah. No, he was laying down on the job. Had Judah been vertical instead of horizontal, his authority would have been properly standing and not lying down.. It became inactive. Inactive authority does not signal danger, because it is not engaged, it is not working. The man mistakenly assumes everything is fine.

The throne is still there; but no one is ruling. We've already learned that vacancy is a terrible thing.

Appetite is such an effective replacement because it's an everyday thing. It doesn't announce a coup. It just answers urgency, manages relief, keeps life moving.

While the man is busy surviving, the mechanisms that would have alerted him to loss never engage. No alarms go off because governance already stopped, like yesterday.

When authority is exercised, it is *aware*. When authority is ordered, it is *protected*. When authority is neglected, it can disappear quietly. Authority that is exercised knows when it is challenged. Authority that is neglected doesn't know when it's gone.

God-given authority protects itself when it is functioning. It only disappears when governance does. There is power protecting the gifts of God.

When David was looking over at the other rooftop at Bathsheba he wasn't USING his gifting just then in the right way and that is when he had more than one malfunction. If he had been at war as he was supposed to be, or at least inside the palace *ruling*, that temptation wouldn't have passed before his eyes. This was lapse through misplacement, not mere temptation.

David's first failure in this case was displacement. The gift and authority that would have protected him was not working because he was out of place and acting like a man of low estate rather than high estate.

In King David's case, Scripture is explicit about timing and posture:

> In the spring, at the time when kings go out to war... David remained at Jerusalem (2 Samuel 11:1)

David wasn't where his authority assignment placed him. David was out of the range of the jurisdiction of his authority at that time. God *sends* people. Being set under authority that's where that delegated (sent) authority will work. Did Jonah have real authority when he went in the opposite direction of what God told him? No, and his disaster was a shipwreck and near loss of many lives. Didn't David's debacle set his bloodline on a course of many lost lives as well? --just over an expanded timeline.

Authority works in a place, a space, and in a time frame.

God *sends* people into assignments, and delegated authority functions only within the boundaries of that sending. When a man removes himself from that jurisdiction, authority does not follow him.

David was meant to be at war, governing, and leading. Instead, he was idle. He was outside the range of his assignment, and that is when authority malfunctioned.

Jonah confirms this law. The same principle appears with Jonah. Jonah did not lose his calling; but he stepped outside its jurisdiction. Jonah's stepping out from authority brough chaos extending beyond himself. Authority misaligned produces collateral damage.

David's consequences were extended into Time. David's failure did not end with Bathsheba. Kingship is generational authority. Therefore, the consequences echoed with violence in his household, rebellion among his sons, and bloodshed within his lineage.

Jonah's disaster unfolded quickly. David's unfolded slowly — across generations.

Different timelines. Same law.

The governing principle is this: authority only functions where it is assigned. Outside that place, discernment dulls—especially when a man is bent on distraction. Restraint weakens, appetite speaks louder, and consequences multiply because jurisdiction has been violated.

A passport, for example, can grant access to many places, but it cannot take you everywhere. Neither does it guarantee the same reception in every place. Authority does not travel with disobedience. When a man leaves his assignment, whether purposefully or he is seduced away, he leaves the protection of its authority. Outside jurisdiction, authority becomes liability and certainly at risk.

They didn't step outside jurisdiction because they *hated* God, they stepped outside because they decided they were *off the clock*; and that is the danger. Jurisdiction is lost the moment a man decides he is unavailable to hear God.

The moment they stopped listening to God, they stopped being positioned. Authority requires ongoing attentiveness to homebase – wherever and whoever homebase is. This is not for occasional obedience.

Authority is lost first by disengaging and then to sin – of course, disengaging is usually for the purpose of sinning. Sin follows disengagement and failure follows after that.

David was not at war, where kings exercised leadership. He was not governing inside the palace with vigilance. Instead, he was idle, disengaged, and unoccupied in authority. And when authority goes idle, appetite gets opportunity.

If David had been using his gifting correctly, the temptation would not have passed before his eyes. *Why?* Because authority filters environment.

When a man is ruling his sight is disciplined, his time is ordered, no time for foolishness. His focus is occupied and his boundaries are active. David already had wives — many of them, so, this was not lack.

It was unguarded authority.

Multiple malfunctions followed one abdication. Once governance lapsed, systems failed in sequence. Sight malfunction – he lingered where he shouldn't. Desire malfunction – appetite spoke without restraint

Authority malfunction – he used kingly power to take, not protect. Justice malfunction – he arranged Uriah's death. Spiritual malfunction – he concealed instead of confessed. One abdication created many sins. And the death spiral in his own family hadn't even started yet. That's the danger of ungoverned authority it doesn't fail just once. Oh no, it cascades. Cascading evil is wickedness.

David may have thought, I'm only looking, but that became so much wickedness that even now we can't forget it.

When sin is ungoverned, it multiplies. When it multiplies, it organizes. When it organizes, it becomes wickedness.

David had escaped death so many times perhaps he was thinking God would always protect him and his offspring. But the system of wickedness that he let into the bloodline said otherwise.

Because temptation looks for idle authority, not righteous desire. David's many wives prove the point that this was not unmet need; it was misplaced governance.

Authority in use protects vision. Authority idle invites intrusion. Appetite does not wait for permission. Temptation exploits vacancy. David didn't fall just because he was weak. He fell because he wasn't ruling at that moment.

Temptation doesn't simply target men in authority it targets moments when authority goes unused. When a king stops ruling, appetite starts looking.

The enemy of our souls is more apt to stay away from authority in motion and is looking for authority that is not in use. (wouldn't that be the same as a person who has a singing gift, for example for worship, but they are not using it so the devil sends someone to "discover' them and the next thing you know they are doing worldly music???

The enemy avoids authority in motion and targets authority that is idle. Authority in Motion Repels Interference. When authority is actively exercised within its assignment, it creates resistance. Not noise, but order.

That's why storms quiet, demons identify rank, temptation reroutes. Authority in motion occupies space, governs time, disciplines attention, narrows access points. There's very little "room" for intrusion. Have you ever considered how many things God has protected you from that just by virtue of the gifting He put in you, your anointing, His Grace and Mercy that you don't even (yet) know anything about?

The enemy does not enjoy contesting active authority; he prefers **vacancy**. Swept, clean, garnished.

Idle authority creates exposure (not sin yet). When authority is not being used, it doesn't disappear. It is simply unguarded. That's the moment when distraction enters, curiosity widens, alternative pathways appear, and "opportunities" show up. Yeah, just what you like. Just what you wished for, daydreamed about. Just what you wanted; custom-made temptations.

The singing gift illustration is a gift that is not exercised under God's authority, not anchored in assignment, not governed by stewardship, becomes available. So the enemy doesn't need to corrupt the gift, He just needs to reassign its platform. Suddenly, someone "discovers" them, the exposure feels affirming, the audience grows, the authority shifts, they get paid – like large. Now, the gift is serving appetite instead of assignment.

Nothing evil happened in one moment.

Authority simply moved — because it was idle.

You may not realize anything evil at all until one day if you are absolutely exhausted and miserable and realize that you are doing this job for money. Maybe just for money, maybe also for fame or power, but you really hate this job. It is not your heart's desire and it does not fulfill you. It may take that long, but that is when you will realize that you traded for appetite. And, it was the appetite of that day because you were broke and tired and hungry.

Still, it may have allowed you to get everything or even more than you ever dreamed of in material goods. But the rich can still be bored. Tremendously bored. So when Solomon says:

"Vanity of vanities, all is vanity,"

he's saying:

*Everything pursued **outside of God's governance** feels substantial while you're reaching for it — and evaporates once you have it.* That includes jobs chosen in survival, paths chosen under pressure, decisions made when hungry, afraid, or exposed. Add to that list, success gained without alignment and provision mistaken for purpose.

Solomon the richest man ever described a life where appetite set direction, desire and urgency replaced discernment, relief was mistaken for calling, and provision was mistaken for fulfillment.

So, the job *worked?* It got you paid; it more than sustained you, and it occupied time. But it never satisfied. A man may come home and blame his dissatisfaction on his wife, his kids, even the dog, but it's not them. That job was not the job of his calling, and it is no one's fault but his own.

One day he breaks up his family to get a different wife and kids. He is making the same mistake again; appetite is choosing for him. Appetite put him in the wrong career and now, even though he could have the right wife and kids, appetite is making him trade them in. This is the danger of a man who does not know God, himself, or his calling.

Solomon, that man and how many others may say, what I sought, I reached it… and it slipped through my fingers.

Why?

Because authority was misaligned. And because the hand cannot hold the greatness that God has put in you.

Solomon called it vanity not because it was useless, but because it was chosen without God. Appetite can build a life that functions perfectly and still feel empty.

Vanity is what remains when appetite chooses, but authority never approved. A life built to survive can still feel meaningless if it was never authorized to rule.

The enemy doesn't just steal gifts to destroy them; he redirects them. The enemy does not create gifts. He does not improve gifts except maybe with gimmicks, sound effects and backup singers that can sing better than the lead. Even if it takes a whole choir he may make you sound really good and you're not even supposed to be a professional singer.

Repositioned authority almost always looks like faster recognition, easier platforms, more money, fewer restraints, *I'm rich and famous now. So, I can do what I want.* immediate reward; all of which appeal directly to appetite.

This isn't about genre; it's about governance. It's about A gift under authority. That gift produces life, creates order, preserves the carrier. A gift under appetite accelerates exposure, increases pressure, consumes the carrier. Same gift, different ruler.

The enemy doesn't fight authority that is being exercised; he waits for authority that is idle.

Better choose a governor or one will be chosen for you.

Whatever a man turns to for relief begins to dictate his schedule, his compromises, his tolerances, and his thresholds. This is why Scripture warns so often about serving "masters." Because appetite never travels alone; it requires allegiance, sooner than later. What feeds you eventually directs you.

Appetite does not want ownership — it wants control. Appetite does not only want to *own* a man; it wants to first manage him, letting him think he is still in charge. Ownership comes later.

First, appetite negotiates time, boundaries, attention and loyalty. Once those are yielded, authority has already changed hands. This is why the most dangerous moments are not dramatic ones; they are the repetitive ones. Even small allowances made under hunger accumulate into governance.

There's a hidden cost. Every time authority is transferred through appetite, something is diminished. Discernment dulls. Patience shortens. Satisfaction fades. The man finds himself needing *more* of what once sufficed. Not because the thing is failing, but because it—that thing was never

59

designed to govern. Appetite cannot stabilize identity. It can only escalate demand.

This feels invisible because appetite feels personal. It feels like preference, coping, self-care, *I deserve this.* It feels like realism. And all this happens quietly, privately. Authority transfers quietly because appetite feels personal.

But governance is still governance, regardless of how gentle the entry feels. This is why men are often shocked when they realize how *owned* they are. They never crossed a visible line. They simply kept agreeing.

Authority does not leave a man all at once. It moves incrementally, decision by decision, toward whatever answers hunger fastest. This is the mechanism. Appetite creates urgency. Urgency demands relief. Relief requires agreement. Agreement transfers authority.

No chains required. No threats necessary. Just hunger without governance. *I do as I please when I please.*

Oh really?

The laws, rules and regulations in the Bible are for our protection, to guard us from exactly this: unseen, insidious things that stalk and trick and steal and kill and destroy. Authority being chief among the things the enemy likes to steal.

Every ungoverned appetite is a point of authority transfer.

Ever see a baby? Everything goes in the baby's mouth. *Why?* Appetite? Curiosity? *I wonder what this is about.* Internal programming? Spiritual inheritance? Appetite is not just about food, fame or money. This is about governance.

EATING THE PASSPORT

If a man is asking about authority His dominant question is: "Who governs this?" He is governed by: order, alignment, stewardship, with consequence-awareness. So, he asks, *"Who set this table?" "What does this require of me later?" "What authority am I yielding by accepting?" "What does this attach me to?"* This man understands something the first man does not: Provision answers hunger. Authority governs outcomes.

A man graduates from asking for provision when he realizes provision without authority is how men are owned.

When appetite outruns authority that will lead to spiritual or other damage. When urgency precedes discernment, that will lead to bondage. When relief replaces governance, that will lead to regret.

The man who asks only for provision will sit at any table. The man who asks about authority chooses his seat, or he leaves.

The man who sees a passport as only paper and words and pictures, who looks to use it for today is different than the man who sees a passport as **authority** and is standing in a different position than it's-only-about-today man.

The first man asks, "What can this get me today?" He sees: ink pages stamps expiration dates To him, the passport is useful only insofar as it can be spent right now. How can it be used for a trip, leveraged for access, cashed in for convenience. This man will misuse it, trade it cheaply, or treat it casually, because he does not understand what it represents.

The second man asks: "What position does this place me in?" He understands: a passport is not paper—it is recognized authority it grants access beyond today it speaks on his behalf where he cannot speak for himself. It places him under protection, jurisdiction, and order. This man does not waste it. He does not burn it to stay warm. He does not patch a hole with it. He knows: Authority is preserved, not consumed.

Those who treat authority as a consumable will always trade tomorrow for today. Those who recognize authority as position can afford to wait. This is why some people spend gifts, some spend access, some spend influence, and some spend favor. They are not wicked.

Appetite uses authority, while Wisdom guards it. Urgency spends it governance preserves it. The man who sees authority as paper will always use it for today. The man who understands authority will protect it for tomorrow.

We have not addressed whether the 'authority' man is thinking yet about eternity, but he is far closer to it than the 'today' man.

Jesus went into the wilderness for forty days and did not eat His passport. With Wisdom and foresight, He refused to consume the very authority that would carry Him beyond the wilderness.

Bread would have solved today Authority secured everything after Jesus understood: Authority is not to be consumed for relief. It is to be preserved for assignment. He didn't starve because of lack of power. He fasted because He refused to misuse that power and authority.

They were being handed a national identity, self-governance, inheritance, priestly calling, freedom from slavery, and they were loaded with spoils.

The Israelites, in their Wilderness – all those millions of people together couldn't figure out what the Mind of Christ could. The Israelites all they wanted to do was eat and be comfortable. Getting into the Promised Land? That was someone else's problem, that was Moses' problem not theirs. (Well their behavior was like this.) Deliverance? *God's problem.* Direction? *Moses' problem.* Provision? *God's problem.* Discomfort? *Everyone else's fault.*

Going back, which was not an option, they were renegotiating in their minds that they would be willing to trade their newfound Authority for food: cukes, melons, leeks, garlic. So what did they take ownership of? **Comfort management.**

If Jesus had eaten His passport, He would not have exited the wilderness. He would have remained provisioned, but uncommissioned. That's the distinction Israel never made. They wanted: relief instead of rule, comfort instead of calling, and food instead of formation. The Bible says that they were sustained, but not transformed. They ate daily... and wandered for forty years.

Jesus did the opposite. He refused to: turn authority into appetite, convert sonship into survival, or spend position to escape pressure. He understood something Israel never fully grasped: Wilderness ends when authority is intact—not when hunger is satisfied.

Provision will keep you alive in the wilderness. Authority is what gets you out. Provision keeps you alive. Authority gets you out. Fulfilling appetite is why people stay stuck even while being sustained, why comfort can delay calling and why appetite can prolong wilderness. Now we can see why Jesus' refusal really mattered. Authority is not lost only by surrender. It is often lost by **consumption**.

This is the mistake men make when appetite is ungoverned: they use what was meant to position them as something to be spent. A passport, of course, is not food; it represents authority. It does not exist to satisfy hunger. It exists to grant access beyond the current border.

But a man who is hungry enough will eat anything.

Authority must be preserved, guarded, and carried forward. It is not consumed for relief. When a man *spends* authority to satisfy appetite, he may survive the moment, but he forfeits movement. He trades future access for present comfort. This is how men remain sustained but stuck. They **eat** what should have carried them out.

Authority answers *where you are going*. Appetite answers *how you feel right now*. When the two are confused, authority becomes expendable and a tragic exchange results. Men begin to say, *I'll deal with the consequences later. This will just help me get through. I can rebuild afterward.* But authority is not easily rebuilt once it has been consumed. A passport eaten in hunger cannot be presented at the border.

Appetite does not recognize authority; it only recognizes **relief**. Authority is abstract until it is exercised. Appetite is immediate. Tangible.

Pressing. So, when pressure rises, men are tempted to use authority as a resource rather than a position.

They spend integrity to maintain access, reputation to secure comfort, calling to preserve convenience, and inheritance to quiet anxiety. They do not call it consumption; they call it survival. This is why the wilderness is such a revealing place. In the wilderness, authority is present, and appetite is loud.

The wilderness is not just a forest, a desert or a place with no roads, or overgrown trails. A wilderness could be your couch where you sit and watch whatever and feed your appetite, swearing you will never act on it. You just want to see it. You just want to know about it. Wow! Other people do that? The Wilderness could be your mind where what is there is projected into whatever device is your favorite or your most used. Your cellphone where you wander and wander and you still don't know how to get out of it or put it down? If you are dedicating that much time to it, better ask, *Does it have my authority?* Or, *Am I still governing myself?*

So, in this wilderness, provision is available, but pressure is intense. The temptation is never simply, *"Are you hungry? Or are you hungry for this? Or this?* It is: *"Will you use authority prematurely to get this that or the other?"* Bread solves today; Authority secures tomorrow and tomorrows.

Provision keeps you alive. Authority gets you **out**. The pattern repeats. Each time authority is consumed for relief: the next decision is harder, the appetite grows louder, the future feels farther away. The man does not realize he is eating his exit.

He believes he is being practical.

Men eat the passport because authority feels *nonessential* under pressure. Hunger convinces them that position can wait, calling can be postponed, order can be restored later. But authority is not a luxury item. It is the very thing hunger cannot replace. Once it is gone, appetite has no answer for movement.

Eating the passport does not produce immediate disaster, another reason why it is so dangerous. The man is still alive; he's still functioning and still provided for. But he cannot cross the border he was meant to pass. He remains inside environments that sustain him but outside the environment that will deliver him. Or better said, outside the environment that marks him as

69

a free man. He remains outside the Promised Land because the path of appetite does not lead him to freedom and autonomy.

Do not follow those breadcrumbs!

That man remains outside of advancement, not because the door is closed but because **he** no longer carries what grants access: his passport--, his authority.

The uncomfortable truth is that men are not trapped because they were denied authority. They are trapped because they had authority but spent it, used it, traded it, lost it. Hungrily. Hunger, once ungoverned, does not distinguish between what may be used and what must be preserved. Hunger wants it now and today.

Relief is not release. Relief will cause a man to eat what was meant to carry them out of where they are wandering and stuck and back into authority.

THE DIFFERENCE BETWEEN RELIEF AND RELEASE

What exactly happened to me?

Relief and release are not the same thing. But hunger makes them feel interchangeable. Relief answers pain. Release answers position. Many men never leave where they are because they confuse the two.

Relief calms. Release moves.

Relief quiets pressure. It soothes discomfort. It stabilizes emotion. Release changes a man's jurisdiction. A man can be relieved and still remain *owned*. He can be sustained and still remain stuck. He can feel better without being positioned differently.

This is why provision alone does not produce progress. But we keep asking for money. Why would you need money if your fingers don't even close? If you can't hold it, .if you can't operate it, if you have holes in your hands, if you have no authority over it? Why are you asking for it?

When a man loses authority, it would be wise for him to know what authority has he lost? Are their levels to this? or does he just lose the authority that would hurt him the most? does he lose the authority that his bloodline is susceptible to?

A man does not lose "all authority" at once. He loses authority in the area where governance was first surrendered, then that loss propagates outward. There are levels; patterns matter. No, it is not random. Nor is it God "targeting" him; it is lawful consequence.

Authority is layered, not singular. Biblically, authority is not a single object you either have or don't have. It is jurisdictional. A man may retain authority in some domains while losing it in others.

Examples: a man may lose clarity of thought, but not appetite. He may lose leadership at work, but not in intimacy. He may suffer loss of discipline in public, but not in private. He may retain spiritual insight, but not self-government. When authority begins to slip, it slips by domain, not wholesale. Authority is lost where governance first failed. This is the governing rule: authority is lost first in the area where restraint was first abandoned. If governance failed at appetite, authority erodes there first. If he lost governance in sexuality, authority erodes there first. And maybe this is why it doesn't work at home anymore. Your spouse is still "hot", it's your **authority** that you laid down and couldn't pick back up. If authority is lost in money, then authority erodes there first. If the infraction was in speech, then authority erodes there first, and no one seems to be hearing you anymore. That is why the loss often feels *personal*, not abstract.

This loss touches the place that was already unguarded.

When authority goes dormant, the man finally experiences the **pressure** it had been holding back.

A man does not lose authority *because* of his bloodline, but ungoverned authority often collapses along familiar family patterns, because those are the areas least reinforced in that bloodline.

So, when authority lapses, it often does so in known grooves, not new ones. Not because the bloodline claims him but because vigilance there was already necessary.

Authority is not taken; it is uncovered. Authority does not leave a man *maliciously*; it leaves functionally. This is like the anointing to use a gift leaves although God does not remove the gift.

The **protection** that authority provided is no longer active. He loses resistance. Things that were once held back now press in.

The loss feels sudden because authority departs quietly, appetite grows gradually, pressure accumulates invisibly. By the time the man notices, the authority has been inactive for a while. The throne wasn't stormed; it was vacated. Authority is lost by domain, not all at once.

A man loses the authority he stopped exercising. Authority lost by neglect can be recovered by order, not force.

It is the area where governance was surrendered that becomes susceptible — not the object itself. The *thing* is incidental. The abdication is the issue. If a man sins with food we see that the appetite domain was ungoverned. When he sins with sex, the desire and intimacy domain was ungoverned. When he sins with

74

money the trust / provision domain was ungoverned. If his mouth is out of control and he sins by speech, his authority of words was ungoverned.

The vulnerability is not because the object is cursed. It's because authority stopped operating there.

The enemy does not waste effort attacking governed territory. He watches for lapses, exploits vacancies, reinforces surrender, and deepens the groove.

So, the enemy does return to the area of non-governance because it's already open. This is why Scripture says, "When an unclean spirit goes out… he returns and finds it swept and put in order…" The enemy returns to where authority was last surrendered. Temptation revisits ungoverned territory. What you stopped governing becomes vulnerable. It's not what you sinned with that stays vulnerable — it's what you stopped ruling.

Provision keeps life going. Release requires intact authority. Relief is so convincing because relief feels like progress because it reduces suffering. Pain decreases. Tension lifts. Breathing and living becomes easier. So, the man assumes *Something has changed.* Something did change. What changed was sensation, not governance.

Relief modifies experience. Release modifies placement. Without that distinction, men can settle for comfort and call it advancement.

Being sustained, but not sent is one of the most subtle traps in Scripture. God will sustain a man that He is still *forming.* He will feed him, protect him, and keep him alive. God will keep that man, even while that man remains uncommissioned. This is Mercy. But Mercy can be misinterpreted. Men begin to believe that sustenance equals approval, relief equals readiness, survival equals progress. So, they mistakenly stop waiting for release.

They adapt. And this is why the Wilderness lasts. The wilderness does not end when hunger is satisfied. It ends when authority is intact or again intact.

This is why manna did not shorten the journey. Quail did not advance the people. Water from the rock did not reposition them. They were relieved repeatedly, over and over again, but never released. They were relieved many times after their murmuring and complaining, but their murmuring and complaining was probably one of the main reasons they weren't released.

God was not unfaithful, but Mercy does not equal release. *"They were relieved repeatedly, over and over again, but never released."*

Murmuring and complaining is evidence of appetite still governing. Complaining is information; it shows who's ruling. This is the law of Relief that is demanded reinforces captivity.

Release comes where governance changes. Their murmuring didn't *cause* God to withhold release, it revealed that authority had not yet been restored.

Relief is temporary. Appetite repeats. Relief answers sensation. Appetite invites urgency. Repetition prevents release. Judges shows us that God can send help repeatedly, and still not release a people who refuse governance.

Repetition in Judges wasn't patience — it was proof that authority kept slipping out of their hands. The Book of Judges is about ungoverned people repeating their cycles over and again. Repetition didn't lead them forward; it only confirmed that authority had never been fully returned.

Release requires governance restored.

Relief Can Delay Formation. Relief interrupts pressure — and pressure is often the environment where authority matures. When relief arrives too early, formation stall because man learns to cope, adapt, survive, how to manage discomfort; how to compensate, but not how to govern.

This is why some people stay functional but do not advance. They are relieved too quickly to be reshaped. *This is good enough. This is better than it was.*

When men confuse relief with release, they stop asking questions, they stop guarding authority, they stop discerning timing. They become content with being sustained inside environments they were meant to exit. They say, *"At least I'm okay,"* when okay is not the goal.

Release is not earned by endurance alone. It requires that authority has not been traded, used up, consumed, exchanged, or reassigned. This is why eating the passport is so devastating. Relief says, *"You feel better now."* which is huge for the man who has been suffering. But release says, *"You are free to go." Freedom means you have agency and authority back.* One soothes the present. The other secures the future.

Many men are not waiting on God to release them. They are waiting on appetite to quiet down. But appetite cannot grant release. It can only negotiate relief which no matter how consistent, does not move borders.

Because appetite keeps repeating... relief is temporary and appetite keeps repeating.

Mustn't we know when the captor is feeding the appetite and not God?

LIARS PROJECT

When the serpent/devil convinced Eve that it wasn't enough, or she was lacking something, or she wasn't "whole" -- he was really projecting because whatever you give him, it's not enough. He's the one who is never satisfied. The serpent projected his own condition onto humanity.

He did not introduce hunger; he introduced dissatisfaction. How could the devil introduce hunger when he is a spirit and he doesn't eat?

The projection is the tell; it always is. The lie in Eden was not, *God is withholding food.* It was, *"What you have (how you've been made) is not enough to make you whole.* Scripture shows that the serpent himself is the unsatisfied one. cast down, restless, unseated, roaming, never at rest. So he speaks from his own condition.

Whatever he touches, he reframes as lacking.

The lie worked because Adam and Eve were provided for, covered, ordered, whole. They had no internal reference for lack. So when the serpent suggested deficiency, it didn't feel false — it felt *informational.*

That's the danger of projection; it doesn't sound like accusation, but it is. And, no surprise, he is the Accuser. But to them and to mankind, it sounds like insight.

Here another law revealed: Wholeness does not need to consume. Lack must always eat again.

The serpent cannot be filled, so he sells *filling* as the solution. We surely know that appetite cannot finish what authority completes. Appetite never ends. Whatever you give him, it's not enough. It's how man gets into trouble with devil deals; no one can ever pay him back. He will ever change the terms of any 'deal' so a man is beholding to him even unto generations. The only way to get out of a devil deal is through a higher authority and that is Jesus Christ. The Name. The Blood. Jesus, the Christ of God.

Appetite is not hunger for provision it's hunger for replacement of authority. And that replacement never satisfies.

The serpent accused God of withholding because he himself is never satisfied. The lie of lack came from one who lives in perpetual lack. He projected his own dissatisfaction and taught man to call it hunger.

The unsatisfied taught the whole to doubt their fullness.

Unto the pure all things are pure: but unto them that are defiled and unbelieving is nothing pure...(Titus 1:15)

Defilement doesn't just corrupt actions, it corrupts interpretation. So the serpent didn't merely lie he spoke as he saw himself and how he saw Creation and all the Universe.

To the whole, fullness is normal. To the defiled, fullness looks suspicious. To the unsatisfied, satisfaction looks fake. So, when he looked at Eden — abundant, ordered, complete, he could only interpret it as *lacking*. Because nothing is ever enough to one who is defiled.

The serpent didn't say to Adam and Eve, *"I am empty."* No, *h*e said, *"You are."* That's projection at its purest form. He reinterpreted, provision as restriction. He said that order as limitation. He convinced them that obedience as deprivation, and wholeness as incompleteness.

Then as he kept saying, *Look, look, look--,* he taught humanity to adopt his lens.

Once defilement governs perception, abundance feels scarce, boundaries feel cruel, authority feels oppressive, restraint feels unsafe. That's how appetite becomes insatiable **without hunger ever being real**.

The serpent didn't introduce sin first. He introduced suspicion of fullness.

Wholeness does not question itself, only defilement does. *That Serpent* could not recognize purity because he no longer possessed it. *That Serpent* had the nerve to say that something God made was not complete-- mankind? womankind? and they believed him. The audacity of the serpent. The Serpent's lie was not merely temptation; it was an accusation against God's work..

He implied that what God declared "very good" was incomplete. Not the garden. Not the food. The humans were made lacking. We know this is not true because we are made in the image and likeness of God.

That Serpent! This is breathtaking nerve.

It worked because the lie wasn't, *"God made you bad,"* but, *"God made you unfinished."* That suggestion strikes at identity, not behavior.

Adam and Eve had never experienced lack, so they had no category for suspicion. They had never heard a lie before. They had never seen a Liar. They didn't know how to evaluate distrust. The Serpent spoke as if he had *insight* they did not and they mistook cynicism for wisdom. So it seems that humanity's first doubt was not about sin. It was about wholeness.

In the Gospels, Jesus asked, **"Wilt thou be made whole?"**

When Jesus Christ asked that question (John 5:6), it was not because the man lacked power to answer. It was because the lie had been living in him for years. That question confronts something deeper than sickness:

Do you still believe you are incomplete? Do you believe wholeness is possible? Or have you made peace with lack?

Jesus wasn't asking about desire. He was testing agreement. Jesus reverses the lie that the serpent told in Eden. The serpent had convinced Eve that she was not whole or complete. This lie gave her/them appetite. Jesus'

84

ministry answers it with a question, *"Will you be made whole?"* In other words, Jesus is asking mankind, represented by that one man, *Will you let Me undo what you agreed with?*

Wholeness was never lost. God did not fail; God has never failed and it is impossible for Him to fail. Truth was obscured because humanity accepted a lie.

The Serpent questioned God's completeness, then humanity questioned its own.

Jesus restores us, even our thinking and our minds by reasserting wholeness, not by shaming lack. Healing in the Gospels is not just repair it is restoration of original design, to factory settings. Those settings were perfect.

The first lie was that man was incomplete, mocking God. Jesus did not come to finish God's work — He came to open blinded eyes.

Lies blind eyes.

WHO YOU CALL LORD

Authority is revealed by address, not by vocabulary, but by governance. In moments of pressure, what a man calls, where he goes, exposes who rules him. Titles are not cosmetic. In Scripture, names and titles are never accidental. They reveal posture. *Teacher* implies learning. *Lord* implies submission. One allows observation, the other requires surrender.

Many are willing to learn, few are willing to be governed. This distinction becomes unmistakable in moments of exposure.

When Jesus announces that one of the disciples will betray Him, the response is immediate. Each disciple asks, *"Lord, is it I?"* The question is not defensive, it is yielded. It assumes authority has the right to search the heart.

Only one man speaks differently. He asks, *"Rabbi, is it I?"* He says, *Teacher*, not *Lord*. That difference is not semantic, it is positional.

Judas reveals in this exchange, possibly without even realizing it is that Judas was willing to learn from Jesus, as a teacher. Judas walked with Him, participated in ministry--, at least marginally. And Judas handled responsibility. But he never reassigned authority to Jesus.

He related to Jesus as a source of instruction, not governance. So, when pressure came, there was nothing to return to. He could regret the outcome. He could confess guilt. He could return money. But he could not return allegiance. You cannot **reassign** authority you never yielded in the first place.

This is about revealing how proximity can mask ownership. Judas was close enough to hear truth, but distant enough to remain governed by appetite. Judas could betray Jesus because something else ruled him more.

Appetite reveals lordship. In moments of hunger, fear, or pressure, lordship surfaces. A governed man asks: *"Lord, what would You have me do?"* An ungoverned man asks: *"What will get* *me through this?"* Both may use spiritual language. Only one has surrendered control.

Who you call Lord is not proven in comfort. It is proven when appetite speaks louder than instruction. Because appetite does not ask permission. It asks for relief. And whatever you obey in that moment is your lord.

WHY SOME NEVER TRANSFORM

Proximity to authority is not the same as being governed by it. This is one of the most dangerous misunderstandings in spiritual life. Proximity feels like safety, progress, and belonging, even when nothing has changed internally.

A man can be close to authority and still remain ungoverned. He can participate, observe, benefit, and still never submit. When proximity replaces governance, ownership quietly persists.

Nearness Feels Like Covering. Being near authority produces secondary benefits. A man near authority may experience protection, provision, access, perks, borrowed credibility, and reflected confidence. These benefits can feel indistinguishable from transformation. But they are not the same. Proximity provides shade. Governance provides structure.

Shade cools discomfort. Structure changes form. Many men choose shade and assume structure will follow. It does not.

Although **p**roximity allows learning, learning is not yielding. A man can hear Truth, repeat language, understand concepts, perform tasks. But learning does not require surrender, governance does. This is why some men grow fluent but never change. They accumulate knowledge without relinquishing control. They know what is right. They simply do not let it rule them.

Proximity allows participation without allegiance or transformation. A man may serve, assist, manage, or even represent authority, and still never yield to it. He may carry responsibility without carrying submission. This produces a dangerous illusion: *"I must be under authority — look at what I'm doing."*

But activity is not alignment.

Service can occur without surrender. Function can continue without governance.

Proximity is seductive because it feels safe. It reduces exposure. A man *near* authority is often shielded from consequence. He benefits from order without enforcing it. He enjoys outcomes without paying the cost of restraint. This is why proximity can last a long time without revealing itself. Things do not collapse immediately, nothing looks wrong, everything seems to function. *Ain't broke, why fix it?*

Well, until pressure comes. Pressure reveals governance. Under pressure, simple proximity fractures. When appetite is activated, governance is exposed.

A man who is governed is different. That man will wait, restrain, submit, protect authority even at personal cost. A man who is merely proximal will negotiate, rationalize, preserve himself, and he will spend authority to relieve pressure. The difference was always there; but it took pressure to make it visible.

Borrowed authority cannot save you and it is never your fit. Proximity allows authority to flow *through* a man, but it does not allow authority to belong *to* him. borrowed authority expires under stress. This is why proximity cannot release a man. It can only delay exposure.

When relief ends, the man is left with what he actually governs — and nothing more.

This is too common. Proximity is easier than governance. It does not require discipline, restraint, identity surrender, or internal reordering. It allows a man to stay intact, and unchanged while still *appearing* aligned.

But unchanged men remain ownable because whatever governs them privately will eventually override what they associate with publicly.

The uncomfortable truth is that many men are not owned because they rebelled. They are owned because they never surrendered. They stayed close, present and even involved, but they never reassigned authority. And you cannot lose what you never yielded.

Proximity to authority may delay consequences. It does not prevent ownership. Only governance does.

THE MONEY MEN

This chapter deals with why some men never transform.

Judas held the money, so I suppose that made him a money man. Not that he had the money or brought the money, but he was in charge of Jesus' ministry's treasury.

When we have a family get together, the one that can't cook is asked to bring the napkins or paper plates. Of the Disciples, many transformed and became apostles and were sent to teach and seek and save and prepare the people.

I am saying the one that may not have been well able to do that was asked to hold the money bag.

Of note, there was a real Disciple that WAS a tax collector. One might think that it would be logical for that man to steward over the ministry's money. No, that man, Matthew became **transformed** under Jesus and became a real disciple, while Judas appears to still be bringing the disposables and sodas to the family BBQ.

In families (and systems), people are often given tasks that match how they are perceived. The one who is trusted with skill, judgment, or growth is given weightier responsibility. The one whose role never changes may be included, but not entrusted. Applying that to the Disciples. The former tax collector (Matthew) had a distorted relationship with money before Jesus, but he was quite familiar and probably comfortable with money and around money.

After Matthew encountered Jesus, he underwent visible transformation left his old system became a steward of Truth and testimony. Matthew's relationship to money was re-governed.

Judas, by contrast, held the money bag complained about "waste" measured value constantly never shows a shift in posture toward authority. Judas ultimately trades Jesus for silver. Now, if Judas was willing to do that, and he needed some money, couldn't he have just asked the ministry for it? Some say he was probably already stealing from the treasury, so couldn't he have just stolen some more? No, that was not his intention.

Judas' internal governance was most likely never changed. Even in families, the one who never learns to cook is forever asked to bring the napkins. Judas held the money, but never matured past disposables.

Meanwhile, the former tax collector was transformed and entrusted with something lasting. Proximity can earn you a task, but it is transformation that earns you trust.

Authority doesn't shift just because access is granted; it shifts when **allegiance** does.

Matthew, in the ministry of Jesus was transformed. He moved from handling money to be entrusted with the **true riches** that Jesus talks about. Without authority men do not transform into **sons** of God and they are not entrusted with true riches.

Transformation is not automatic. Time does not guarantee it. Exposure does not guarantee it. Just showing up or participation does not guarantee it. Some people remain unchanged not because they lacked opportunity, but because they never surrendered governance.

Transformation requires reassignment. transformation is not improvement. It is reassignment of authority. A man is transformed when something else is finally allowed to rule him. This is why information alone does not change people. Knowledge can illuminate, but it cannot govern.

A man may know the truth and still refuse to let it command him. Transformation begins where authority changes hands.

Proximity Can Delay Change. Some remain untransformed precisely because they are close enough to function. There is an office manager that I know who works very well with others because she delegates to them all day long. When they don't understand something, or say they don't she "shows them." She shows them the same thing over and over and yet they never learn. They are close enough to her for her to 'cover' them and make them look like they know what they are doing; but they do not. It is not until this manager goes on vacation that they all fall flat on their faces.

Proximity provides structure without surrender. It can give benefit without cost. In it is protection without discipline. So, there is no immediate need to change.

As long as things "work," the inner world remains untouched.

This is why some stay around authority for years and never grow. They adapt externally while remaining internally sovereign.

Saul was in the company of prophets one day and because of the anointing on them and Saul's proximity he also began to prophesy. Saul was not a prophet, but he functioned in that gifting because he was in the company of prophets.

Appetite preserves the old self as you keep doing the same things you used to do the same old way you always did it.

Transformation, on the other hand, threatens appetite. To change is to lose familiar comforts, predictable coping, and self-managed relief. So appetite resists transformation not with rebellion, but with reason. It says:

- *"Now is not the time."*

- *"You can change later."*

- *"This isn't necessary."*

And because appetite feels urgent, it is obeyed.

The man stays the same — not because he is unwilling to change, but because he will not relinquish control over how he is comforted. More—*ain't broke* excuses.

Then there's the myth of gradual surrender. Many believe transformation will happen slowly, painlessly, over time, without a decisive yielding. Scripture shows that transformation requires a moment of governance shift. The Words say, on the day of provocation, harden not your heart. Jesus wept over Jerusalem because they missed the day of their visitation. He did not say season or year, or three years, He said day. That surrender is made by decision, right then.

Without that moment, growth stalls.

The man may modify behavior, manage image, or adopt language — but the core remains intact.

Some may appear to change but they really haven't. Some men look transformed because circumstances change. Pressure lifts.

Provision increases. Environment improves. But if authority never shifted, the old governance reasserts itself the moment pressure returns. This is why relapse is so common.

The issue was never willpower. It was lordship. Some never transform because transformation would cost them their favorite *idol*. Some are willing to learn. They are willing to serve. They are willing to stay close, and even show up for every meeting and crusade.

However, they are not willing to yield. Without yielding, nothing truly changes. Transformation does not happen because Truth is present, it happens because authority is reassigned. Until that occurs, proximity produces familiarity — not sonship.

TRUE RICHES ARE RARE

True riches are rare because they require sons. Scripture does not speak of true riches as rewards for effort. It speaks of them as entrustments. That language matters. Something entrusted is given to one who has demonstrated governance. True riches are not earned by effort; They are entrusted to sons.

Sonship requires governance.

Many handle money, influence, or responsibility, but few are entrusted with authority that multiplies life. Without transformation, entrustment would destroy them. God withholds out of much Wisdom.

Jesus makes a clear distinction between Mammon and true riches.

Mammon can be managed.

True riches must be **carried**.

Mammon responds to skill, strategy, and opportunity.

True riches respond to alignment.

This is why many can handle money, influence, or access — yet few are entrusted with authority that produces life in others.

True riches are weighty; they are not neutral. Without governance, they crush instead of bless.

Being entrusted with true riches requires **sonship.**

A servant may complete tasks. A son abides in the house forever. A son guards the house. He is more like a shepherd than a hireling. A servant, whether paid or not is a hireling in that his basic needs are met.

True riches are not transactional; they are relational. They require identity stability, restraint, and long obedience.

A man who has not settled who governs him cannot be trusted to govern others. So, God does not rush entrustment. Not because He is slow but because authority given too early becomes appetite fuel.

Many who would-be sons plateau at competence. They learn systems. They manage processes. They execute responsibilities. Only competence is not sonship. Without sonship, authority would be misused, maybe or maybe not maliciously, but definitely hungrily. So, God allows some to remain functional but untrusted. Alive. Active, but not expanded.

True riches are screened for by pressure which reveals what a man obeys, what he preserves, what he sacrifices. Under pressure, appetite and authority compete. Whoever wins determines readiness. This is why wilderness seasons precede entrustment. They are not delays; they are examinations.

From the outside, this may feel unfair. Some seem gifted but limited. Some seem capable but constrained. Some seem faithful but unseen. Scripture shows that entrustment is not based on visibility. It is based on governance. God is not impressed by output. He is attentive to order.

If lost, true riches cannot be recovered easily. God is a forgiving God, but the conditions that caused loss must be addressed. Authority is not reclaimed by apology alone. It is restored through reordered allegiance. That process takes time. This is why true riches are guarded carefully.

Many want the fruit of true riches without the restraint that it takes not to misuse them. They want true riches without the constraints that preserves them. They want impact without surrender. Influence without obedience. Authority without order.

Scripture is consistent: True riches belong to **sons**, and **sons** are governed. True riches are rare because few are willing to be reordered deeply enough to carry them.

Refer to the previous chapter where we discussed the money men.

Some want miracles without lordship – Simon the Sorcerer wanted access without sonship. Simon the Sorcerer is a clear example of a man who wanted access without sonship. He believed, he followed, and he even stayed close to the apostles — but when he saw that the Holy Spirit was given through the laying on of hands, his appetite spoke. He offered money for the ability to dispense power, not realizing that authority cannot be purchased, transferred, or imitated without alignment. Simon did not ask to be governed; he asked to be enabled. He wanted proximity to power without submission to process, influence without transformation, results without relationship. Peter's rebuke exposes the issue plainly: Simon's heart was not right, because he sought authority as a tool rather than as a trust. This is the danger of appetite dressed as belief — it recognizes power, but refuses sonship. And without sonship, authority will always be misused or lost.

He wanted what sons carry, but he did not want to become one.

What many people do is collection, not consecration. They are showing that they don't want to be *formed*; they want to be *assembled*. They become samplers. A gift from here, a blessing from there, a revelation from this stream, a technique from that one. None of this is for the purpose of being governed, that is set under authority, but it is to optimize themselves.

That impulse says:

- *"I'll take the parts I like."*

- *"I don't need the altar, just the oil."*

- *"I don't need sonship, just access."*

- *"I don't need authority, just outcomes."*

That's appetite, folks. That is appetite masquerading as spirituality. Curating gifts without governance produces spiritual hoarders. It's the same error as:

- Simon wanting the laying on of hands

- Judas wanting access without lordship

- Esau wanting satisfaction without stewardship

- Israel wanting manna without movement

Ungoverned appetite turns inheritance into a shopping list. People curate gifts when they refuse to submit to formation.

Sonship receives what the Father gives, in order. Appetite selects what it wants, out of order, out of governance. And that's the danger: what is gathered without governance cannot be sustained —

WHEN CREATION RESPONDS

Creation responds to authority before men do. Creation does not flatter. It does not pretend. It does not negotiate. It responds.

Creation is not waiting for activity. Scripture says that creation waits for the manifestation of the sons of God. Not their intentions. Not their language, nor their effort; but their appearing. Creation is not waiting for belief systems or declarations. It is waiting for governance restored.

Creation was placed under stewardship. Disorder reveals absence of stewardship. When authority is fractured, creation reflects it. When this happens, land resists, systems strain, cycles distort and even the behavior of things created becomes erratic.

Creation reacts.

This is why Scripture repeatedly links human authority with environmental response. Blessing is not mystical; it is order working as designed. When sons are absent, creation groans.

Not because it hates man, but because it was designed to respond to him.

Creation knows before we do. Creation was created by the Spirit, and it serves God in Truth. There is no other way it can react. It responds to what *is*. Period.

When true sons of God mature and authority is restored, creation settles. Noise quiets. Patterns normalize. Resistance eases. Naturally.

Authority produces rest which is not inactivity; it is right order. When authority is intact, Creation is allowed to do what it was designed to do — cooperate. This is why Sabbath is not first a rule, but a signal. It signals that governance is in place.

This is similar to when a woman marries a man who is in order she is allowed then to be totally and completely a woman. It is her joy.

Creation rests when sons are rightly positioned because nothing is being asked to compensate for misrule.

The healing of Creation is evidence that sons of God have appeared. Healing follows authority the way shadows follow form. It is not summoned; it is revealed. This is why miracles are signs — not tricks.   They testify that order has been restored in at least one place.

Sons and Creation bear witness together. Sons do not announce themselves; Creation does; Creation announces the sons of God. When authority is exercised without appetite, without urgency, without self-protection, Creation recognizes it immediately. Jesus did not argue with storms. He spoke, and they obeyed. The storm recognized order. This is why Peter's shadow healed; Peter has become a true son of God.   Creation does not respond to hunger. It responds to governance. It does not obey desperation. It yields to authority. And this is the quiet confirmation that sons have appeared. When creation no longer strains to compensate for disorder.

Creation is not waiting for men to become powerful. It is waiting for them to become governed.

SONS AND STEWARDSHIP

Sonship is not proven by inheritance alone. It is proven by stewardship. In Scripture, sons are not merely identified by who they belong to, but by what they are entrusted with, and how they carry it.

Stewardship is the evidence of sonship A servant may manage tasks. A son is entrusted with outcomes. Stewardship assumes continuity. It assumes care beyond the moment. It assumes that what is handled today must still be whole tomorrow.

This is why authority and stewardship are inseparable. A man who cannot steward what is placed in his care reveals that he is not yet positioned as a son, regardless of proximity, gifting, or language.

Authority is not a possession, it is responsibility. Sons do not consume what they inherit. They preserve it, multiply it, and guard it. Authority in a son does not look like control; it looks like restraint. It looks like patience. It looks like the ability to delay gratification in order to protect what has been entrusted.

This is why sons are not reckless with influence, access, or power. They understand weight. Stewardship without governance collapses into exploitation.

When appetite rules, stewardship becomes extraction instead of care, use instead of preservation, consumption instead of cultivation. But when authority is intact, stewardship becomes natural.

The son does not ask, *What can I get?* He asks, *What must be protected?* That question alone reveals governance. The difference between access and entrustment is that many have access, but few are entrusted. Access allows presence, entrustment requires reliability.

God does not entrust what He intends to last to those who are still negotiating with appetite. That's not because they are unworthy but it is because stewardship requires settled authority.

Sons think generationally. Stewardship forces time to widen. A son does not think only about survival. He thinks about continuity. As said earlier, he may not be thinking of Eternity yet, but the man with the raging appetite is not thinking generationally or of Eternity at all.

A stewarding *son* asks things like, *What happens after this season? Who will be affected by this decision? What does this establish?* This is why sons are often slower to move, quieter in speech, and less reactive under pressure. They are stewarding; they are guarding something.

At the same time, true stewardship is rarely dramatic. It looks like consistency, restraint, patience, and quiet responsibility. To those who have an appetite for drama, it looks boring. This is why it is often overlooked.

Creation recognizes it. Creation knows when order stabilizes, and when systems cooperate. And Creation knows when resistance diminishes. Stewardship leaves fingerprints long after appetite has given up and moved on because it realizes that it will not be assuaged.

Sons do not prove themselves by asserting authority. They prove themselves by how they care for what authority touches.

Stewardship, unmistakable evidence of sonship.

SONS OF GOD

For the earnest expectation of the creature
waiteth for the manifestation of the sons of
God. (Romans 8:19)

"Creature" here means *creation* — all that was
made

"Earnest expectation" means *strained, forward-
leaning anticipation*

"Manifestation" means *revealed, made visible,
made evident* — not appointed, not crowned, not
announced

Creation is not waiting for sons of God to **exist** —
they already do

Creation is waiting for them to appear as who they
are.

Paul's argument in Romans 8 is that
Creation is stuck in frustration because

governance is delayed until sons mature enough to steward it.

Things are out of order.

Heavens and Earth created. Something happened then there was darkness and void over the face of the deep. then Adam and Eve messed it up—now it's broken again.

It's something like God saying, I'll help you but now *you'd* better fix it.

Creation is waiting for the Sons of God to appear. AND when Creation is "healed" that is proof that the sons of God have matured and appeared.

Cosmic Stewardship / Creational Order

This is the governing idea behind Epistle to the Romans 8.

Creation and humanity are linked by assignment, not sentiment. Man was given dominion (Genesis 1). Creation was placed under stewardship of man. When stewardship fractures, Creation reflects it. (Hey, this man is not doing his job.)

The Earth as a witness

In Scripture, God repeatedly calls heaven and earth to witness human choices and covenant faithfulness.

- *"I call heaven and earth to record this day against you..."* (Deut. 30:19)

- *"Hear, O heavens, and give ear, O earth..."* (Isa. 1:2)

This means Creation is treated as a legal witness to obedience or rebellion. What happens on the Earth is not private; it is *registered* in God's order.

The Earth reacts to what is done on it. Blood "cries out from the ground" (Cain and Abel). The land becomes cursed because of sin. The ground "vomits out" inhabitants because of defilement (Leviticus). Creation groans under misuse and waits for rightful governance (Romans 8)

This tells us that human authority affects the condition of the earth.

When stewardship is restored, creation responds. So, Creation's healing is evidence of mature sons, not merely blessing. Creation does not respond to titles. It responds to rightful governance.

Authority exists before it is visible. But only manifested authority produces order.

Outcomes testify to maturity. In Scripture, healing testifies to rightful authority. Order testifies to governance. Fruit testifies to alignment.

Creation being healed is the witness that sons of God have appeared. How many? Well, at least two so we have a plurality. When sons mature, creation stabilizes. When sons appear, creation responds. This is why Jesus didn't argue authority — He demonstrated it, and nature obeyed.

Creation waits for the sons of God to appear. And when creation is healed, it is proof that the sons have appeared.

Creation's healing is not the cause of sonship — it is the evidence of it. That is order restored.

Throughout Scripture and nature alike, abnormal behavior in Creation shows up when order is fractured, governance is distorted, boundaries are violated, authority is misaligned. When rightful authority is restored, Creation doesn't need to *signal* anymore. Not because Creation was "confused," but because **it was reacting to disorder**. Creation doesn't rebel; it **responds**.

Creation and sons are paired testimonies, mutual witnesses.

Here's the clean way Scripture holds it:

Creation and sons as reciprocal witnesses. Creation bears witness to the state of governance. Sons bear witness to the state of maturity. They testify to one another. When sons mature, Creation responds. When creation stabilizes, it testifies that *sons* have appeared.

Manifestation always produces effects.

AUTHORITY IS ALWAYS ORDERED

Authority does not exist in isolation. It exists in order. Many, when they think about authority: they imagine it as power possessed rather than position held. But Scripture presents authority as something that functions only when it is rightly aligned.

Authority that is not ordered does not disappear, it malfunctions. Authority flows through alignment. Biblically, authority flows downward through submission, not upward through assertion.

A man does not gain authority by standing alone. He gains it by being rightly positioned under a higher authority. This is why the centurion could recognize Jesus instantly. He understood rank. He understood command. He understood that authority is not proven by presence, but by order.

"I am a man under authority…"

That sentence is not humility language. It is jurisdictional clarity. Authority without order becomes force. When authority is detached from order, it becomes coercive.

It demands rather than directs. It pressures rather than positions. It consumes rather than governs. This is why ungoverned authority produces fear instead of peace, chaos instead of stability, and resistance instead of cooperation.

Order is what allows authority to operate without violence. God will not bypass order; He does not circumvent His own design. He does not grant authority to those unwilling to be governed, not because He withholds, but because authority outside order destroys both the carrier and the environment.

This is protection — not punishment. When authority is prematurely exercised, it feeds appetite rather than establishes stewardship.

So, God insists on order first. sons are placed, not self-appointed. Sons do not announce themselves. They are put in positioned and named for that position.

Placement requires order. It requires timing. It requires alignment. This is why self-appointed authority is always unstable. It lacks covering. It lacks continuity. It lacks legitimacy.

True authority does not need to assert itself. It is recognized. Creation recognizes it. People recognize it. Systems respond to it.

Because order is present.

Disorder reveals misalignment and it reveals the source. When authority is claimed but chaos increases, order has been bypassed.

When leadership exists but nothing stabilizes, authority has been severed from governance. This is not a mystery. It is evidence. Authority that produces peace is ordered. Authority that produces fear is not.

The test questions apply again and again:

- Does authority create rest?
- Does it preserve what it touches?
- Does it endure pressure without compromise?

If not, order is missing. Authority is never proven by activity. It is proven by what remains stable when pressure comes.

Authority is not freedom from restraint. Authority is the result of restraint rightly applied. That is why sons wait. That is why stewardship precedes expansion. That is why appetite must be governed before authority can be trusted.

Authority is always ordered, or it will not last.

WHAT MATURITY LOOKS LIKE

Maturity is not the absence of hunger; everyone knows a man has to eat. But maturity is the presence of mind when hunger arises.

A mature man does not obey every impulse automatically. He pauses. He discerns. He asks whether this hunger is physical, emotional, spiritual, or circumstantial. He considers consequence. He considers tomorrow. He considers whether his feet belong under that table.

This is not anxiety. This is governance.

Maturity is not denial, numbness, or hyper-discipline. It is Wisdom guiding desire. It is knowing that you are under authority, and therefore you conduct yourself accordingly. A man in authority is always set under authority. He does not go rogue when no one is looking.

He understands that the authority he carries only functions within the boundaries assigned to him.

This is why the centurion astonished Jesus. He understood order. He understood that authority works through alignment, not proximity.

"For I also am a man set under authority…"

That sentence reveals maturity.

A mature man does not rush. He is not impulsive. He is not careless with appetite. The Lord is his Shepherd; he does not want — not because nothing is available, but because nothing is missing.

He may encounter desire. He may feel temptation. But he does not panic.

Mature governance assures that even when hunger comes that man does not act irrationally because he knows he will not die. He does not enter survival mode. He maintains composure, remembering who he is and whose he is. If I pass on this desire, this hunger, what will happen to me?

This is what governance looks like before freedom moves.

This is the presence of governance.

The Centurion asked Jesus that the Centurion's servant who was at home be healed. Jesus was on the way to the man's house to heal, but the Centurion said something very faithful and telling.

... the centurion sent friends to him, saying unto him, Lord, trouble not thyself: for I am not worthy that thou shouldest enter under my roof: Wherefore neither thought I myself worthy to come unto thee: but say in a word, and my servant shall be healed. **For I also am a man set under authority, having under me soldiers, and I say unto one, Go, and he goeth; and to another, Come, and he cometh; and to my servant, Do this, and he doeth *it.*** When Jesus heard these things, he marvelled at him, and turned him about, and said unto the people that followed him, I say unto you, I have not found so great faith, no, not in Israel. (Luke 7:6b-9)

Being under authority means that you have the rights and privileges that have been released to you by your superior. If you abuse those privileges, the person whose authority you are under can strip you of those rights. Not because they are evil, but usually it is to protect you. And, usually it is to protect you from hurting others or even yourself.

The man who governs appetite doesn't rush. He is not impulsive. He is not careless. The

Lord is his Shepherd; he does not want. He doesn't feel that there is anything missing, nothing broken. He is not craving food, fame, power, money, life, or *experiences*. This person is settled and satisfied. He does not lack; he does not want. He has learned in whether abased or abundant to not worry or fear. He knows the Word and he cannot be enticed to turn his back on it.

I know what it is to be in need, and I know what it is to have plenty. I have learned the secret of being content in any and every situation, whether well fed or hungry, whether living in plenty or in want. (Philippians 4:12)

Even if he is in a wilderness temptation, he will say, like Jesus in His own wilderness temptation, "It is written...", and he will not cross that threshold into sin.

Maturity is the ability to remain whole in the presence of unmet desire.

He knows that hunger may arise; but he won't die, therefore he is not thrust into survival mode. He maintains his composure, knowing who he is and whose he is.

YOU DON'T EXIT BY EATING

The days are coming,' declares the LORD, 'when
I will bring my people Israel and Judah back
from captivity and restore them to the land I
gave their ancestors to possess,' says the
LORD.(Jeremiah 30:3)

No one leaves captivity by consuming
more. However, looking for more, reaching for
more is the final deception appetite offers. Man
believes that if he is more comfortable then he is
closer to freedom. Just a little more relief, one
more concession will eventually become release.

It will not.

Eating your feelings won't get you out.
Eating your emotions won't get you out of any
trouble. Receiving comfort won't get you out of
captivity of any kind. Jesus resisted the
temptations in the Wilderness and THEN the
angels came and ministered to Him; not before.

Eating does not move borders. It stabilizes presence inside them. This is why men remain in places that sustain them but do not advance them. They keep eating what allows survival while consuming what would have carried them out, or having traded the thing that would have gotten them out for relief or comfort.

Appetite is not a strategy. It answers pain and quiets discomfort. It responds to urgency. But it does not know where you are going. So, when appetite leads, movement stalls. A man who eats his way through pressure may remain alive, but he does not become free.

This is where it really gets complicated: **more** provision doesn't work. Provision answers hunger, not governance. More provision reduces pressure, increases tolerance and lengthens stay. It does not restore authority.

This is why God can continue to provide for people who are not moving. Provision is mercy. It is not permission. Movement requires something else. Many men are not waiting for God to open a door. They are waiting for appetite to quiet down. But appetite never quiets if you keep feeding it or giving in to it. It will never quiet permanently, anyway; it must be told what to do. It must be governed. When you govern your appetite, you govern yourself. When you can govern yourself, you can govern your environment. When you can govern your environment then your domain is under your authority. Now you can be identified as a son of God. It can only be restrained. And restraint is an authority act.

You don't exit by eating. You exit by not eating what compromises authority. This is not punishment. It is positioning. And until this is understood, nothing else will matter.

Before restraint, Esau traded his birthright, but the blessing was stolen by Jacob and Rebecca's manipulations. Scripture treats those two acts very differently. There were two transfers, two mechanisms. Esau sold his birthright voluntarily. He was hungry. He despised (treated as light) what he already possessed. He consented to the exchange.

Thus, Esau despised his birthright, (Genesis 25). This is appetite-driven surrender. No deception, force, or theft. Esau *chose relief over responsibility*. Ungoverned hunger transfers authority willingly.

Jacob & Rebekah took the Blessing by deceptive seizure. The blessing was not sold. It was taken through manipulation. Rebekah orchestrated it. Jacob impersonated Esau. Isaac was deceived. This is not appetite. This is premature grasping. The blessing involved inheritance confirmation, future authority, spoken destiny, and it was obtained out of order.

Scripture condemns one more than the other. Esau is warned against and cited negatively in the New Testament because: he treated sacred authority as expendable. he normalized trading inheritance for appetite. That's why Hebrews 12 calls him "profane."

Jacob, by contrast, is corrected, disciplined, renamed, wounded, and governed over time. His sin wasn't indifference, it was impatience. Both were wrong. But they were wrong in different categories. One birthright was surrendered by appetite. The other blessing was seized by manipulation. One is voluntary loss. The other is illicit acquisition.

You can lose authority by despising it; you can delay destiny by grasping for it early. Esau lost what he had. Jacob suffered for taking what was promised, but not yet authorized. Esau gave authority away cheaply. Jacob took destiny unlawfully. Different errors. Different consequences. Same lesson: Authority must be active and governed, not traded, exchanged, or dormant. **AMEN.**

A Prayer to Reclaim Authority

Father God,
In the Name of Jesus Christ. I acknowledge
You as the source of all authority.
I acknowledge that authority is given, not
taken; stewarded, not consumed.

Today, I repent for every place where
appetite governed instead of Wisdom,
where urgency spoke louder than obedience,
where comfort replaced calling,
and where I surrendered authority without
realizing it.

Where I yielded ground through fear,
hunger, distraction, impatience, or survival
thinking, or through misplaced gratitude,
I now **withdraw that consent**.

I renounce every agreement — spoken
or unspoken that transferred my authority to
appetite, to systems, to people,
to fear, to urgency, or to relief.

I declare that my authority was never
destroyed — only misplaced.

And by Your Mercy and order, I now
return it to its rightful alignment under You.

Father, restore me to the place You assigned me. Restore my discernment. Restore my restraint. Restore my jurisdiction.

I ask for return of **governance, clarity, right order. I ask not for** relief but for release.

Where my authority was dulled, sharpen it. Where it was abandoned, re-establish it. Where it was misused, correct it. Where it was stolen, recover it.

I declare: I will no longer eat my authority through the appetites that are common to man or peculiar to me. Lord, deliver me from wrong appetite. I will no longer trade inheritance for relief.
I will no longer confuse provision with permission.

I receive the grace to govern myself, to wait without consuming, to desire without surrendering, to stand without scrambling.

I take my seat again — under You, within my assignment, in the domain You entrusted to me.

And I declare by faith: Authority has returned. Order is being restored. My appetite will serve Wisdom — not rule it.

In Jesus' Name, Amen.

Daily Declaration

**I reclaim my authority under God.
My appetite does not rule me.
My assignment defines my actions.
I govern myself with Wisdom, restraint, and clarity.**

In the Name of Jesus, Amen.

I seal these words decrees, declarations and prayers across every dimension and timeline, past, present, and future, to infinity, in the Name of Jesus.

I seal them with the Blood of Jesus and the Holy Spirit of Promise.

Any retaliation against this author, the reader or anyone who prays these prayers, makes these decrees and declarations at any time, let that retaliation backfire on the head of the perpetrator to infinity, and without Mercy, in the Name of Jesus.

Dear Reader

Thank you for acquiring and reading this book, **Ungoverned Hunger:** *How Unchecked Appetite Dismantles Authority*

Shalom,

Dr. Marlene Miles

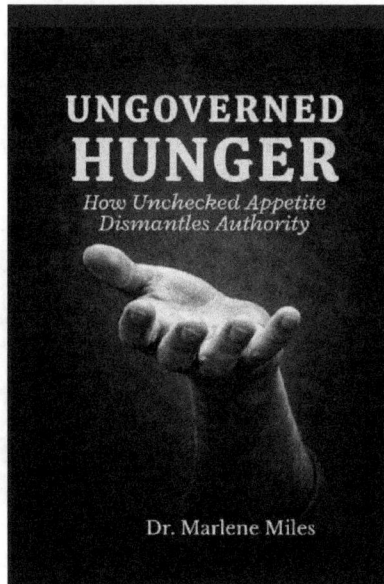

Prayerbooks by this author

There are some books that are only prayers. You just open up the book and pray.

Prayers Against Barrenness: *For Success in Business and Life*

Fruit of the Womb: *Prayers Against Barrenness*

Beauty Curses, *Warfare Prayers Against*
https://a.co/d/5Xlc20M

Courts of Marriage: Prayers for Marriage in the Courts of Heaven *(prayerbook)*
https://a.co/d/cNAdgAq

Courtroom Warfare @ Midnight *(prayerbook)*
https://a.co/d/5fc7Qdp

Demonic Cobwebs *(prayerbook)* https://a.co/d/fp9Oa2H

Every Evil Bird https://a.co/d/hF1kh1O

Gates of Thanksgiving

Spirits of Death, Hell & the Grave, Pass Over Me and My House

Throne of Grace: Courtroom Prayer

Warfare Prayer Against Poverty https://a.co/d/bZ61lYu

Prayer Books by this Author

Prayer Manuals

FAKE FRIENDS: *Prayers Against Betrayers*

HOLIDAY WARFARE Prayer Manual (humorous) Surviving Family Gatherings All Year Long (without catching a case)

SOUL TIE Prayer Manual (The) Part of a 3-part series including a workbook.

MAD at DADDY Prayer Manual – part of a 3-part series including a workbook.

Healing the Sibling & Relative Wound Prayer Manual

Healing the Father-Son Wound Prayer Manual

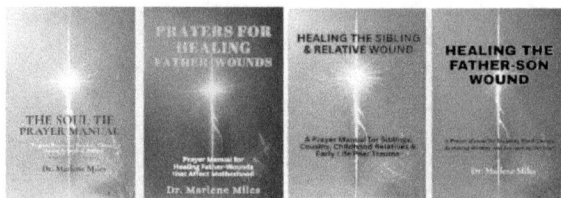

Prayers Against Barrenness: *For Success in Business and Life*

Breaking Curses of the Mother Prayer Manual

Other books by this author

Abundance of Jesus (The)
https://a.co/d/5gHJVed

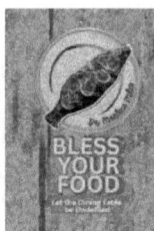

Blindsided: *Has the Old Man Bewitched You?* https://a.co/d/5O2fLLR

Break Free from Collective Captivity

Broken Spirits & Dry Bones

By Means of a Whorish Father

Caged Life: Get Out Alive!
https://a.co/d/bwPbksX

Casting Down Imaginations

Christ of God (The) 3-book series

Christ of God, Box Set, includes all three books

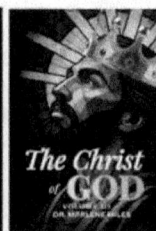

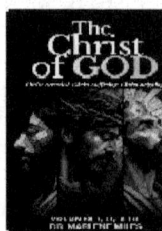

Churchzilla, The Wanna-Be, Supposed-to-be Bride of Christ https://a.co/d/eAf5j3x

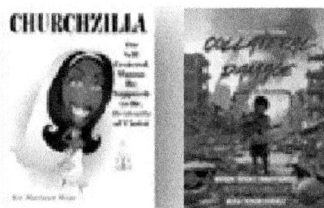

Collateral Damage: *When What Happened Spiritually Was Your Fault*

Demonic Cobwebs (prayerbook)

Demonic Time Bombs

Demons Hate Questions

Devil Loves Trauma, *The*

Devil Weapons: Unforgiveness, Bitterness,...

The Devourers: Thieves of Darkness 2

Do Not Swear by the Moon

Don't Refuse Me, Lord (4 book series)
https://a.co/d/idP34LG

Dream Defilement

The Emptiers: *Thieves of Darkness, 1*
https://a.co/d/5I4n5mc

Evil Touch

Failed Assignment

Fantasy Spirit Spouse
https://a.co/d/hW7oYbX

FAT Demons (The): *Breaking Demonic Curses* https://a.co/d/4kP8wV1

The Fold (5-book series)

- The Fold (Book 1)
- Name Your Seed (Book 2)
- The Poor Attitudes of Money (3)
- Do Not Orphan Your Seed (4)
- For the Sake of the Gospel (5)
- My Sowing Journal

Gang Ups: Touch Not God's Anointed

Gathered: No Longer Scattered
https://a.co/d/1i5DPIX

Getting Rid of Evil Spiritual Food

https://a.co/d/i2L3WYQ

got HEALING? Verses for Life

got LOVE? Verses for Life
https://a.co/d/8seXHPd

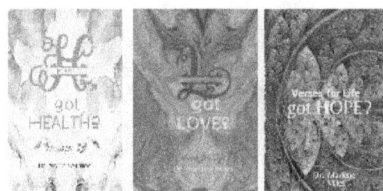

got HOPE? Verses for Life

got money? https://a.co/d/g2av41N

Has My Soul Been Sold?
https://a.co/d/dyB8hhA

Here Come the Horns: *Skilled to Destroy*
https://a.co/d/cZiNnkP

Hidden Sins: Hidden Iniquity

https://a.co/d/4Mth0wa

How to Dental Assist

How to Dental Assist2: Be Productive, Not Wasteful

How to STOP Being a Blind Witch or Warlock

I Take It Back

Irresistible: Jesus' Triumphal Entry
https://a.co/d/d09IfEC

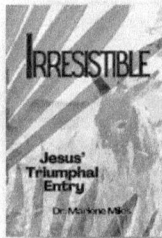

Legacy

Let Me Have A Dollar's Worth
https://a.co/d/h8F8XgE

Level the Playing Field

Living for the NOW of God

Lose My Location https://a.co/d/crD6mV9

Love Breaks Your Heart

Mad At Daddy: Healing Father-Wounds that Affect Motherhood (book, workbook & prayer manual)

Made Perfect In Love

Mammon https://a.co/d/29yhMG7

Man Safari, *The*

Marriage Ed. Rules of Engagement & Marriage

Made Perfect in Love

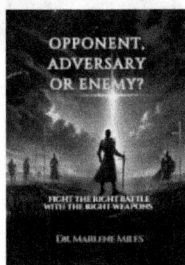

Powers Above

The Robe, Part 1, The Lessons of Joseph

The Robe, Part II, The Lessons of Joseph

Seasons of Grief

Seasons of Siege: GOD IS COMING

Seasons of Waiting

Seasons of War

Second Marriage, Third--, *Any Marriage*
https://a.co/d/6m6GN4N

Seducing Spirits: Idolatry & Whoredoms
https://a.co/d/4Jq4WEs

Shut the Front Door: *Prayers to Close Portals*
https://a.co/d/cH4TWJj

Sift You Like Wheat

Six Men Short: What Has Happened to all
the Men?

SLAVE

Sleep Afflictions & Really Bad Dreams
https://a.co/d/f8sDmgv

Soul Prosperity soul prosperity series 3

https://a.co/d/5p8YvCN

Soul Ties: How Soul Ties Form, and How To Break Them (book, workbook & prayer manual)

Souls Captivity soul prosperity series 2

The Spirit of Anti-Marriage

The Spirit of Poverty
https://a.co/d/abV2o2e

Spiritual Thieves https://a.co/d/eqPPz33

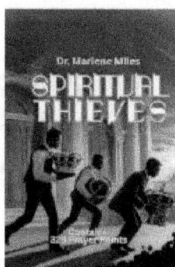

StarStruck- Triangular Power series.

SUNBLOCK- Triangular Power series.

The Swallowers: *Thieves of Darkness*, 3

Take It Back

This Is NOT That: How to Keep Demons from Coming at You

Time Is of the Essence

Too Many Wives: *Why You Have Lady Problems*

Tormenting Spirits https://a.co/d/dAogEJf

Toxic Souls

Triangular Power *(series),* Powers Above, SUNBLOCK, Do Not Swear by the Moon, STARSTRUCK

Unbreak My Heart: *Don't Let Me Die*

Uncontested Doom

Ungoverned Hunger: Unchecked Appetite

Unguarded Hours, *The*

Unseen Life, *The* (forthcoming)

Upgrade: How to Get Out of Survival Mode Toxic Souls (Book 2 of series) , Legacy (Book 3 of series)

The Wasters: *Thieves of Darkness,* Bk 2
https://a.co/d/bUvI9Jo

What Have You to Declare? What Do You Have With You from Where You've Been?

When I Was A Child, *I Prayed As a Child*

When the Devourer is Rebuked

https://a.co/d/1HVv8oq

When the Table Is set Against You

WTH? Get Me Out of This Hell
https://a.co/d/a7WBGJh

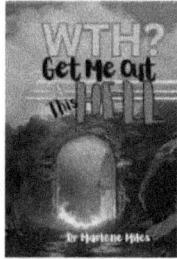

The Wilderness Romance *(series)* This series is about conducting a Godly relationship and marriage with someone who is a Wilderness person. It is about how to recognize it and navigate through it. These books are about how not to get caught up in such.

- *The Social Wilderness*
- *The Sexual Wilderness*
- *The Spiritual Wilderness*

Other Series

The Fold (a series on Godly finances)
https://a.co/d/4hz3unj

Soul Prosperity Series https://a.co/d/bz2M42q

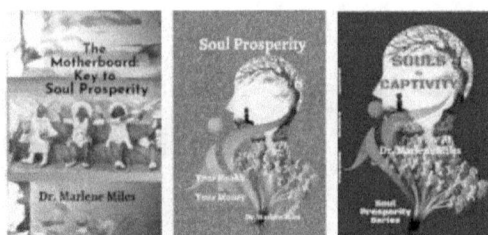

Spirit Spouse books

https://a.co/d/9VehDSo

https://a.co/d/97sKOwm

Battlefield of Marriage, The

https://a.co/d/eUDzizO

Players Gonna Play

https://a.co/d/2hzGw3N

Sent Spirit Spouse (can someone send you a spirit spouse? This book is not yet released.)

Matters of the Heart, Made Perfect in Love
https://a.co/d/70MQW3O , Love Breaks Your Heart https://a.co/d/4KvuQLZ, Unbreak My Heart https://a.co/d/84ceZ6M Broken Spirits & Dry Bones https://a.co/d/e6iedNP

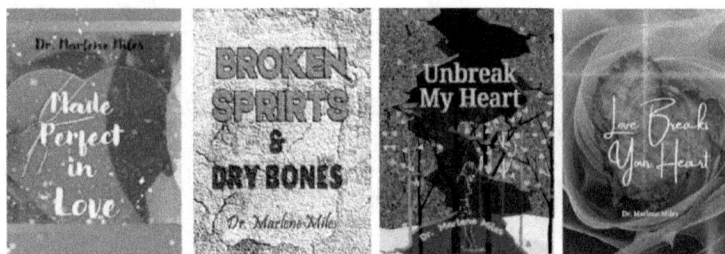

Thieves of Darkness series

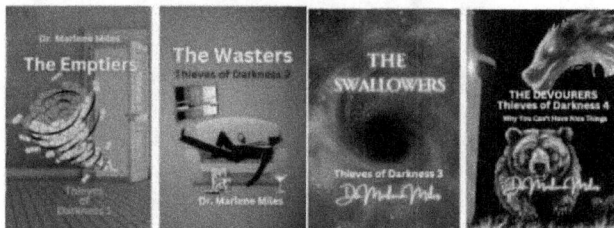

The Emptiers https://a.co/d/heio0dO

The Wasters https://a.co/d/5TG1iNQ

The Swallowers https://a.co/d/1jWhM6G

The Devourers: Why We Can't Have Nice Things https://a.co/d/87Tejbf

Spiritual Thieves

Triangular Powers https://a.co/d/aUCjAWC

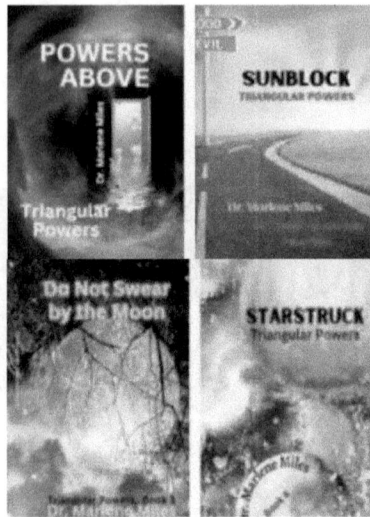

Upgrade (series) *How to Get Out of Survival Mode* https://a.co/d/aTERhXO

We Get Along, Right? Compatibility for Couples – (book & workbook)

www.ingramcontent.com/pod-product-compliance
Lightning Source LLC
LaVergne TN
LVHW052028080426
835513LV00018B/2222